AQA A-LEVEL
ENGLISH
LANGUAGE
PRACTICE TEST PAPERS

SARAH CARPENTER

Contents

PRACTICE EXAM 1

Paper 1: Language, the Individual and Society 3

Paper 2: Language, Diversity and Change 13

PRACTICE EXAM 2

Paper 1: Language, the Individual and Society 19

Paper 2: Language, Diversity and Change 29

Answers 34

Acknowledgements

The author and publisher are grateful to the copyright holders for permission to use quoted materials and images.

Cover and page 1: © Shutterstock.com/Napat

Every effort has been made to trace copyright holders and obtain their permission for the use of copyright material. The author and publisher will gladly receive information enabling them to rectify any error or omission in subsequent editions. All facts are correct at time of going to press.

Published by Letts Educational
An imprint of HarperCollinsPublishers
1 London Bridge Street
London SE1 9GF
ISBN: 9780008276232

First published 2018

10 9 8 7 6 5 4 3 2 1

British Library Cataloguing in Publication Data.

A CIP record of this book is available from the British Library.

Commissioning Editor: Gillian Bowman
Author: Sarah Carpenter
Project Management: Mark Steward
Copyediting: Louise Robb
Proof checking: Rachel Hamar
Cover Design: Sarah Duxbury
Inside Concept Design: Ian Wrigley
Text Design and Layout: Jouve India
Production: Natalia Rebow
Printed in the UK

The author would like to thank Jessica Carpenter, Elizabeth Carpenter and Minnie McManus for writing some of the child language texts.

Pages 5-6, reproduced by permission of NHS.uk; page 7, 'Female Recipe Book; Or, Modern Companion for the Ladies... by an Experienced Matron', estimated to be published 1818, London; page 16, 'Allow me to womansplain the problem with gendered language' by Arwa Mahdawi, 23 April 2017 © Guardian News & Media Ltd 2018; page 17, 'The 'sexist' words your children are no longer allowed to use at school' by Helena Horton, 19 October 2015 © Telegraph Media Group Limited 2013/2015; page 21, 'Queen's 90th birthday celebrations mark her love of horses' by Caroline Davies, 15 May 2016 © Guardian News & Media Ltd 2018; page 22, *A Relation of the Late Royall Entertainment Given by the Right Honourable the Lord Knowles, at Cawsome House neere Redding: to our most Gracious Queen, Queene Anne, in her progresse toward the Bathe* (London, 1613) © British Library Board (C.21.c.48); page 32, 'Young people of the internet: can you not (write properly)?' by Fay Schopen, 28 December 2014 © Guardian News & Media Ltd 2018; page 33, 'Twerking, selfie and unlike? Young people don't speak like that – I should know' by Isabelle Kerr, 28 August 2013 © Telegraph Media Group Limited 2013/2015.

Name: ....

Practice Exam 1

ENGLISH LANGUAGE

Paper 1: Language, the Individual and Society

Time allowed: 2 hours 30 minutes

Instructions

- Use black ink or black ball-point pen
- There are **two** sections:
  - – Section A: Textual Variations and Representations
  - – Section B: Child Language Development
- Answer **all** questions from Section A
- Answer **either** Question 4 **or** Question 5 from Section B
- Write down all of your rough work. Cross through any work that you do not want to be marked.

Information

- The maximum mark for this paper is 100
- The marks for questions are shown in brackets
- There are 25 marks for Question 1, 25 marks for Question 2, 20 marks for Question 3, and 30 marks for **either** Question 4 **or** Question 5
- You will be marked on your ability to:
  - – use good English
  - – organise information clearly
  - – use specialist vocabulary where appropriate.

Advice

- It is recommended that you spend 30 minutes reading and preparing the texts. In Section A, it is recommended that you spend 30 minutes writing your Question 1 answer, 30 minutes writing your Question 2 answer and 20 minutes writing your Question 3 answer. It is recommended that you spend 40 minutes writing your Section B answer.

Section A

Textual Variations and Representations

Answer **all** questions in this section.

Text A – is a page from the NHS.uk website accessed on 2 January 2018.

Text B – is an extract from a 'Female Recipe Book', published in 1818 (estimated).

[0|1] Analyse how **Text A** uses language to create meanings and representations.

[25 marks]

[0|2] Analyse how **Text B** uses language to create meanings and representations.

[25 marks]

[0|3] Explore the similarities and differences in the ways **Text A** and **Text B** use language.

[20 marks]

Text A

Sore throats are very common and usually nothing to worry about. They normally get better by themselves within a week.

How to treat a sore throat yourself

To help soothe a sore throat and shorten how long it lasts you can:

- gargle with warm salty water (children shouldn't try this)
- drink plenty of water – but avoid hot drinks
- eat cool or soft foods
- avoid smoking or smoky places
- suck ice cubes, ice lollies or hard sweets – but don't give young children anything small and hard to suck because of the risk of choking
- rest.

How to gargle with salt water

A pharmacist can help with sore throats

To help relieve the pain and discomfort of a sore throat you can:

- use <u>paracetamol</u> or <u>ibuprofen</u>
- use medicated lozenges or anaesthetic sprays (although there's little proof they help).

You can buy them from a supermarket or from a pharmacist without a prescription.

Find a pharmacy

See a GP if:

- your sore throat doesn't improve after a week
- you often get sore throats
- you're worried about your sore throat
- you have a sore throat and a very high temperature, or you feel hot and shivery
- you have a weakened immune system – for example because of diabetes or chemotherapy.

Home   About   Articles   Help   Login

Book a GP appointment online

Antibiotics

GPs don't usually prescribe antibiotics for sore throats because they won't relieve your symptoms or speed up your recovery.

Causes and symptoms of sore throats

Sore throats are usually caused by viruses (like cold or flu) or from smoking.

Symptoms include:

- painful throat especially when swallowing
- dry scratchy throat
- redness in the back of the mouth
- bad breath
- mild cough
- swollen neck glands.

The symptoms are similar for children, but children can also get a temperature and appear less active.

Conditions that can cause a sore throat

Call 999 if:

- you have difficulty swallowing or breathing
- you're drooling
- your voice changes pitch or becomes wheezy
- your symptoms are severe and getting worse quickly.

These symptoms can make breathing more difficult.

Call 111

If you can't speak to your GP or don't know what to do next.

Lumps in the Throat or Glands, from Cold.

If they hurt internally, drink a table spoonful of warm milk, with a great deal of pepper in it, wash it down with warm milk, rub the outside with sweet oil and spirits of hartshorn, and wrap up very warm. This, if only arising from a cold will have the wished for effect, but if from scurvy, it is necessary to bathe the lumps with strong salt and water several times a day, and to apply leeches frequently; take Ether's mineral in treacle, which you can get properly mixed at the chemist's, three or four spoonfuls every morning, and wear a piece of vervain root at the stomach, suspended round the neck by a ribbon. If you find the tumour disperse, proceed with patience and perseverance, and the cure though slow, will be sure. If you find it still hard, increase, or inflame, do not trifle with it, but seek professional skill. An elderly woman of respectability, well known to the Compiler of this Work, was the widow of a medical man; after his decease, she added materially to her income, by the sale of a medicine for the scrofula, or King's evil, which she sold at 2s. 6d. the wine bottle—a gill to be taken every morning, fasting, and once a week a dose of Epsom salts; three or four bottles have in general cured the most obstinate cases.

Section B

Child Language Development

Answer **either** Question 4 **or** Question 5 in this section.

EITHER

0 4   'More Knowledgeable Others play a major part in child language development.'

Referring to Data Set 1 in detail, and to relevant ideas from language study, evaluate this view of children's language development.

[30 marks]

Transcription Key:

(.)	Pause of less than a second
(2)	Longer pause (number of seconds indicated)
Bold	Stressed syllables
[*italics*]	Contextual information
CAPITAL LETTERS	Raised volume
//	Phonemic transcription
{}	Simultaneous speech

Phonemic Reference Sheet

Monophthongs

iː see /siː/	ɪ sit /sɪt/	ʊ good /gʊd/	uː two /tuː/
e egg /eg/	ə away /əweɪ/	ɜː her /hɜː/	ɔː four /fɔː/
æ cat /kæt/	ʌ up /ʌp/	ɑː ask /ɑːsk/	ɒ on /ɒn/

Diphthongs

ɪə here /hɪə/	eɪ eight /eɪt/	
ʊə cure /kjʊə/	ɔɪ boy /bɔɪ/	əʊ no /nəʊ/
eə there /ðeə/	aɪ my /maɪ/	aʊ now /naʊ/

Consonants

p pen /pen/	b bee /biː/	t ten /ten/	d do /duː/	tʃ chair /tʃeə/	dʒ just /dʒʌst/	k can /kæn/	g go /gəʊ/
f five /faɪv/	v very /verɪ/	θ thing /θɪŋ/	ð this /ðɪs/	s so /səʊ/	z zoo /zuː/	ʃ she /ʃiː/	ʒ pleasure /pleʒə/
m me /miː/	n nine /naɪn/	ŋ long /lɒŋ/	h house /haʊs/	l love /lʌv/	r right /raɪt/	w we /wiː/	j yes /jes/

ʔ
glottal stop

Data Set 1

Jessica (J) is 5 years old, Lizzy (L) is 3 years old. Their mother (M) is recording their conversation at the dinner table. They have been to school (Jessica) and pre-school nursery (Lizzy) during the day.

J   Were you in were you the special helper in the morning and the afternoon?

L   I not in that /dat/ I not gonna /dɒnə/ (2) not gonna /dɒnə/ have that /yat/ when I when I jus go to nursery and be a special helper. On Sundays mummy what day is it today?

M   Today's Friday

L   Uh I only going /dəʊin/ to be um a special helper when it's Friday

J   Was it your first time being the special helper?

L   Yeah

J   {I thought}

L   {Yesterday I might} be a special helper

J   Tomorrow [*tone indicates correction of L's utterance*] (2) You mean Monday (1) you might be the special helper again

L   Yeah

J   But I definitely /defintli:/ know that you're not the special helper do two days in a row

M   You're right, that's right somebody else might have a turn on Monday

(5) [*Lizzy attempts to peel a banana*]

L   Mummy can't /ta:nt/ do it

J   You say 'I can't do it yet'(.) I can't do it yet

L   Lizzy can't do it yet (.) Lizzy can't do it yet

J   Because (3) the actually there's no 'I can't do it' allowed on our (.) in my school

M   Really? What do you say?

J   I can't do it yet (.) or I can't do it I'm going to keep on trying

Source: Private Data

OR

0 5   'Children prefer to focus on the content of their writing rather than accurate spelling.'

Referring to Data Set 2 and Data Set 3 in detail, and to relevant ideas from language study, evaluate this view of children's language development.

[30 marks]

Data Set 2

Jessica is 5 years and 1 month old. She produced this writing independently at home.

when I whent to

lunden my

favit thing waz gowin

on the bot

Data Set 3

Jessica is 5 years and 1 month old. She produced this writing at home, asking a parent how to spell 'Christmas' and 'Nativity'.

at christmas i

I was a star and

I wos in the

nativity play

Practice Exam 1

ENGLISH LANGUAGE

Paper 2: Language, Diversity and Change

Time allowed: 2 hours 30 minutes

Instructions

- Use black ink or black ball-point pen
- There are **two** sections:
  - Section A: Diversity and Change
  - Section B: Language Discourses
- Answer **either** Question 1 **or** Question 2 from Section A
- Answer **both** Question 3 **and** Question 4 from Section B
- Write down all of your rough work. Cross through any work that you do not want to be marked.

Information

- The maximum mark for this paper is 100
- The marks for questions are shown in brackets
- There are 30 marks for **either** Question 1 **or** Question 2, 40 marks for Question 3 and 30 marks for Question 4
- You will be marked on your ability to:
  - use good English
  - organise information clearly
  - use specialist vocabulary where appropriate.

Advice

- It is recommended that you spend about 45 minutes writing your Section A answer. You should spend 15 minutes preparing the material for and 45 minutes writing your answer to Question 3 and 45 minutes writing your answer to Question 4.

Section A

Diversity and Change

Answer **ONE** question in this section.

EITHER

0 1 Evaluate the idea that powerful people use powerful language.

[30 marks]

OR

0 2 Evaluate the idea that language change is beyond prescriptive jurisdiction.

[30 marks]

Section B

Language Discourses

Answer **both** Question 3 **and** 4 in this section.

| 0 | 3 | Text A is the start of an article from the Guardian online on gendered language. Text B is an article from the Telegraph online about gendered language.

Analyse how language is used in Text A and Text B to present ideas about gendered language. In your answer you should:

- examine any similarities and differences you find between the texts

- explore how effectively the texts present their views.

[40 marks]

| 0 | 4 | Write a feature article about young people's language use in which you assess the ideas presented in Text A and Text B and argue your own views.

[30 marks]

Allow Me to Womansplain the Problem with Gendered Language

Arwa Mahdawi

Words such as 'girlboss' and 'manspreading' have gone from making an important point to reinforcing the differences between men and women

Sun 23 Apr '17 19.59 BST Last modified on Sat 25 Nov '17 03.11 GMT

She is a #Girlboss. She is a mumtrepreneur. She is a SheEO. He is a manterrupter. A mansplainer. A manspreader. He is always bropropriating women's ideas. She is a feminazi. He's got a dadbod and the man flu. What is it with the growing popularity of overtly gendered neologisms? From chick flicks to dick pics, from boss babes to guyliner, there has been a proliferation of his or hers portmanteaux.

Much of this is feminism's fault, naturally. There has been more scrutiny of everyday sexism; words such as manspreading and manterrupting simply give a name to behaviour that was taken for granted before. There has also been more discussion of women in the workplace, leading to a rise in supposedly empowering labels such as girlboss, a term popularised by Sophia Amoruso, the founder of online retailer Nasty Gal. In 2014, Amoruso wrote a bestselling memoir/self-help book for entrepreneurially minded millennial women called #GIRLBOSS and the word entered the popular vernacular – it is now a Netflix show.

Neologisms such as girlboss and SheEO are supposed to be tongue-in-cheek, of course. They are supposed to illuminate the fact that words such as boss and CEO are not actually gender-neutral, but implicitly coded as male, that language is "man made", as the feminist Dale Spender put it, and reinforces a male world view. However, I can't help feeling that, when it comes to girlboss, that subtlety has been lost. There are 5,491,625 pictures tagged with #girlboss on Instagram. It has become a cutesy girl-power phrase that is less empowering than it is patronising. It doesn't tear down the sexism encoded in language, it reinforces it.

The same is true of the manifold vocabulary for manshaming. Words such as manspreading or mansplaining are – or at least they were – useful. If you don't have a name for something, then it is harder to talk about and it is taken less seriously. But mansplaining and the various other man-words have become overused and diluted. They have gone from making an important point to simply being lazy ways to reinforce gender binaries. Men are like this; women are like that.

◄ ► + https://www.... ↻ 🔍

| Home | About | Articles | Help | Login |

The 'sexist' words your children are no longer allowed to use at school

Teachers are to be issued guidelines from the Institute of Physics detailing the words which are to be banned from the playground

By Helena Horton

9:05AM BST 19 Oct 2015

Children as young as five are going to be admonished for using language that enforces gender stereotypes as new guidelines are sent to every school in England this Tuesday.

School students are no longer allowed to use **sexist language** to bait each other in the playground, such as "man up" and "go make me a sandwich", and head teachers are being urged to ensure that sexist language is taken as seriously as racist language.

Photo: Shutterstock

These guidelines come from a report by the Institute of Physics.

In response, some schools are creating volunteer squads of girls to police sexist attitudes and report back to teachers.

Schools are also being asked by the report to appoint senior teachers as 'gender champions', appointing them with the task of encouraging more girls to take traditionally 'male' subjects such as economics, computer science and physics at GCSE and A-level and more boys to take 'female' subjects such as English literature, foreign languages and psychology.

Stereotypes are blamed for the fact that there is a **gender divide** in the subjects taken at GCSE and A-level. Only 19 per cent of girls who scored an A* in GCSE physics studied it at A-level in 2011. This contrasts to the amount of boys - just under half of whom scored an A* in physics studied it at A-level in the same year.

Boys are twice as likely to study maths, three times as likely to study further maths and more than four times as likely to take A-level physics.

The stereotypes hold true with the 'female' subjects as well; twice as many girls studied English A-level as boys in 2014 while 70% of psychology A-level students were women.

Clare Thomson, of the Institute of Physics, who helped to draw up the guidelines, told The Sunday Times: "Even low-level comments are potentially an issue with teachers using phrases such as 'man up'."

The subject choice gender divide has been **partially blamed for the pay gap** - women currently earn 19 per cent less per hour than men, as the 'female' subjects are often thought of as 'soft' subjects and tend to lead to lower-paid careers.

Research funded by the Department for Education in 10 schools found that where there was a pattern of girls choosing 'female' GCSE subjects there was often also a wider culture of sexist attitudes and language.

An assessment of the pay gap is being led by **Nicky Morgan**, the education secretary, who is also minister for women and equalities.

These new 'gender policies' have been piloted in a selection of schools already before being rolled our across the country.

Janice Callow, deputy head of one of the pilot schools - Fairfields High School in Bristol, told the Sunday Times: "We have always had clear policies on racist language but now we are making it clear to staff that any kind of sexist language is not acceptable," she said.

"We used to say 'Man up, cupcake'. We've stopped that. Saying 'Don't be a girl' to a boy if they are being a bit wet is also unacceptable. Language is a very powerful tool. You have to be so conscious of what you are saying to children."

BLANK PAGE

Practice Exam 2

ENGLISH LANGUAGE

Paper 1: Language, the Individual and Society

Time allowed: 2 hours 30 minutes

Instructions

- Use black ink or black ball-point pen
- There are **two** sections:
  - Section A: Textual Variations and Representations
  - Section B: Child Language Development
- Answer **all** questions from Section A
- Answer **either** Question 4 **or** Question 5 from Section B
- Write down all of your rough work. Cross through any work that you do not want to be marked.

Information

- The maximum mark for this paper is 100
- The marks for questions are shown in brackets
- There are 25 marks for Question 1, 25 marks for Question 2, 20 marks for Question 3, and 30 marks for **either** Question 4 **or** Question 5
- You will be marked on your ability to:
  - use good English
  - organise information clearly
  - use specialist vocabulary where appropriate.

Advice

- It is recommended that you spend 30 minutes reading and preparing the texts. In Section A, it is recommended that you spend 30 minutes writing your Question 1 answer, 30 minutes writing your Question 2 answer and 20 minutes writing your Question 3 answer. It is recommended that you spend 40 minutes writing your Section B answer.

Section A

Textual Variations and Representations

Answer **all** questions in this section.

Text A – is a page from the Guardian website.

Text B – is an extract from a published retelling of the entertainments laid on for the Queen by Lord Knowles in 1613.

| 0 | 1 | Analyse how **Text A** uses language to create meanings and representations.

[25 marks]

| 0 | 2 | Analyse how **Text B** uses language to create meanings and representations.

[25 marks]

| 0 | 3 | Explore the similarities and differences in the ways **Text A** and **Text B** use language.

[20 marks]

Text A

| Home | About | Articles | Help | Login |

Queen's 90th birthday celebrations mark her love of horses

TV and pop royalty meet the real thing as no fewer than 900 horses join the birthday celebrations at Windsor Castle

By Caroline Davies

Even the Queen's well-documented love of horses must have been sated by the equine extravaganza staged as part of her 90th birthday celebrations on Sunday.

No fewer than 900 – 10 for each of her years – paraded and pranced for her delectation at Windsor Castle during a birthday gala that also included a brace of dames in actor Helen Mirren and singer Shirley Bassey.

TV royalty Ant and Dec welcomed the top tier of constitutional royalty – the Queen with the first and second in line to the throne – to the party in which even the myriad horses were outnumbered by 1,500 human riders and performers, including 600 from the military and some household-name special guests.

Appropriately, the Queen and the Duke of Edinburgh, 94, arrived in the horse-drawn Scottish state carriage.

Other highlights of the show, televised live on ITV, were 13-year-old Kinvara Garner, from north Wales, who played a horse-obsessed teenage Princess Elizabeth as part of a re-enactment of Queen's life with set pieces from her birth, the second world war, her marriage and coronation.

Performers included singers James Blunt, Gary Barlow, Beverley Knight and Kylie Minogue from the world of pop. There was no visible evidence of the Queen wearing ear plugs as she had done at Buckingham Palace pop concerts staged to celebrate her Golden and Diamond Jubilees.

In its unusual combination of regimental marching, gun salutes, pop, historical clips outlining an ABC of the Queen's life history, and Shetland ponies dashing to actor Imelda Staunton's singing "Sing Sing Sing Sing", the show was a unique homage.

Staunton's husband Jim Carter, who played Downton Abbey butler Carson, narrated as the King's Troop Royal Horse Artillery proved their display mettle, and singer Alfie Boe stoked wartime memories by singing the Vera Lynn classic A Nightingale Sang in Berkeley Square.

Katherine Jenkins delivered the patriotic I Vow to Thee My Country, and a choir version of the coronation anthem Zadoc the Priest also filled the arena and actor Martin Clunes appeared as president of the British Horse Society.

In his gala programme address, Prince Charles said: "As we marvel at the incomparable skill of rider and horse alike, we might allow our minds to drift to Xenophon's observation that "a horse is a thing of beauty ... none will tire of looking at him as long as he displays himself in his splendour".

He added he hoped everyone watching would "join with me in wishing my mother, the Queen, the happiest of very special birthdays".

A RELATION OF
THE LATE ROYALL
ENTERTAINMENT GIVEN BY

the Right Honorable, the Lord K N O VV L E S,
at *Cawsome*-House neere *Redding* : to our
most gracious Queen, Queene A N N E,
in her Progresse toward the *Bathe*
vpon the seuen and eight and
twentie dayes of Aprill.
1613.

Or as much as this late Entertainment hath beene much desired in writing, both of such as were present at the performance thereof, as also of many which are yet strangers both to the busines and place : it shall be conuenient, in this generall publication, a little to touch at the description and situation of Cawsome seate. The house is fairely built of bricke, mounted on the hill-side of a Parke, within view of Redding, they being seuered about the space of two miles. Before the Parke-gate, directly opposite to the House, a new passage was forced through earable-land, that was lately paled in, it being from the Parke about two flight-shots in length : at the further end whereof, vpon the Queenes approch, a Cynick appeared out of a Bower, drest in a skin-coate, with Bases of greene Calico, set thicke with leaues and boughes : his nakednesse being also artificially shadowed with leaues ; on his head he wore a false haire, blacke and disordered, stucke carelessely with flowers.

Section B

Child Language Development

Answer **either** Question 4 **or** Question 5 in this section.

EITHER

| 0 | 4 |

'The use of questions has a significant impact on a child's acquisition of language.'

Referring to Data Set 1 in detail, and to relevant ideas from language study, evaluate this view of children's language development.

[30 marks]

Transcription Key:

(.)	Pause of less than a second
(2)	Longer pause (number of seconds indicated)
Bold	Stressed syllables
[*italics*]	Contextual information
CAPITAL LETTERS	Raised volume
//	Phonemic transcription
{}	Simultaneous speech

Phonemic Reference Sheet

Monophthongs

i: see /si:/	ɪ sit /sɪt/	ʊ good /gʊd/	u: two /tu:/
e egg /eg/	ə away /əweɪ/	ɜ: her /hɜ:/	ɔ: four /fɔ:/
æ cat /kæt/	ʌ up /ʌp/	ɑ: ask /ɑ:sk/	ɒ on /ɒn/

Diphthongs

ɪə here /hɪə/	eɪ eight /eɪt/	
ʊə cure /kjʊə/	ɔɪ boy /bɔɪ/	əʊ no /nəʊ/
eə there /ðeə/	aɪ my /maɪ/	aʊ now /naʊ/

Consonants

p pen /pen/	b bee /bi:/	t ten /ten/	d do /du:/	tʃ chair /tʃeə/	dʒ just /dʒʌst/	k can /kæn/	g go /gəʊ/
f five /faɪv/	v very /verɪ/	θ thing /θɪŋ/	ð this /ðɪs/	s so /səʊ/	z zoo /zu:/	ʃ she /ʃi:/	ʒ pleasure /pleʒə/
m me /mi:/	n nine /naɪn/	ŋ long /lɒŋ/	h house /haʊs/	l love /lʌv/	r right /raɪt/	w we /wi:/	j yes /jes/

ʔ glottal stop

Data Set 1

Lucy (2 years and 6 months) is playing in the garden with her mother (M)

M   What are you doing Lucy?

L   I want to go /dəʊ/ in the car

M   Go on then

L   In the car

M   What are you going to do?

L   Um

M   What is it?

L   It a turner it go /dəʊ/ like this

M   It's a turner? Are you turning it?

L   Yeah

M   Lovely

L   Now I can /tan/ drive

M   And now you can drive?

L   Yeah

M   Where will you drive?

L   Um, to a slide /sjaɪjd/

M   to the slide /slaɪjd/?

L   Yeah

M   Go on then

L   Can /tan/ you lift /jɪf/ me up here?

M   Ok

L   I think it not driver up here

OR

0 5   'Children's creative writing is more detailed than factual writing.'

Referring to Data Set 2 and Data Set 3 in detail, and to relevant ideas from language study, evaluate this view of children's language development.

[30 marks]

Data Set 2

Minnie is 5 years and 7 months old.

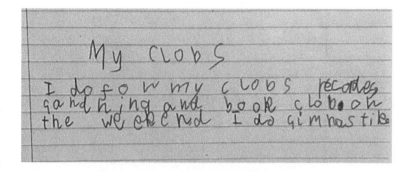

My Clobs

I do for my clobs recordes
gardning and book clob. on
the weekend I do gimnastiks

Data Set 3

Minnie is 5 years and 6 months old.

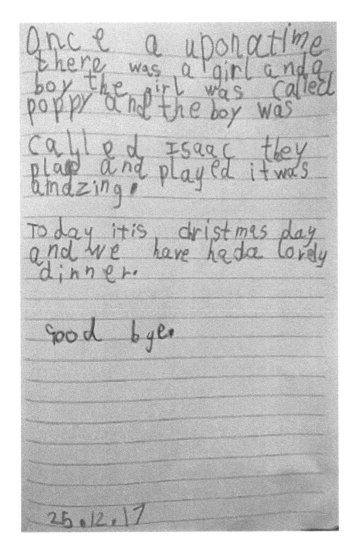

Once a uponatime
there was a girl and a
boy the girl was called
poppy and the boy was

called Isaac they
playd and played it was
amazing.

Today itis christmas day
and we have hada lovely
dinner.

Good bye.

25.12.17

BLANK PAGE

Practice Exam 2

ENGLISH LANGUAGE

Paper 2: Language, Diversity and Change

Time allowed: 2 hours 30 minutes

Instructions

- Use black ink or black ball-point pen
- There are **two** sections:
  - Section A: Diversity and Change
  - Section B: Language Discourses
- Answer **either** Question 1 **or** Question 2 from Section A
- Answer **both** Question 3 **and** Question 4 from Section B
- Write down all of your rough work. Cross through any work that you do not want to be marked.

Information

- The maximum mark for this paper is 100
- The marks for questions are shown in brackets
- There are 30 marks for **either** Question 1 **or** Question 2, 40 marks for Question 3 and 30 marks for Question 4
- You will be marked on your ability to:
  - use good English
  - organise information clearly
  - use specialist vocabulary where appropriate.

Advice

- It is recommended that you spend about 45 minutes writing your Section A answer. You should spend 15 minutes preparing the material for and 45 minutes writing your answer to Question 3 and 45 minutes writing your answer to Question 4.

Section A

Diversity and Change

Answer **ONE** question in this section

EITHER

0 1 Evaluate the idea that social groups use language in order to exclude others.

[30 marks]

OR

0 2 Evaluate the idea that prescriptive attitudes are detrimental to language development.

[30 marks]

Section B

Language Discourses

Answer **both** Question 3 **and** 4 in this section.

0 3   Text A is an article from the Guardian online on young people's language use. Text B is the start of an article from the Telegraph online about young people's language use.

Analyse how language is used in Text A and Text B to present ideas about how young people use language. In your answer you should:

- examine any similarities and differences you find between the texts
- explore how effectively the texts present their views.

[40 marks]

0 4   Write an opinion article about young people's language use in which you assess the ideas presented in Text A and Text B and argue your own views.

[30 marks]

Young people of the internet: can you not (write properly)?

Fay Schopen

I love words. But the language the kids use in tweets, Instagram posts or Snapchats, the talk of 'baes' and 'feels' … I can't even

Sun 28 Dec '14 11.00 GMT Last modified on Tue 21 Feb '17 18.17 GMT

Once you start, it's hard to stop thinking of things you'd love to see the back of in 2015. <u>Men wearing buns</u>, the <u>Cereal Café</u>, Russell Brand, people's opinions of Russell Brand … I could go on, but I realise that there is something I hate much more, all over the internet: words. Not just any words, but the language young people use in tweets, Instagram posts, Snapchats and whatever else the kids do online these days.

Words like "bae", which I discover to my horror has been <u>added to the Oxford Dictionary this year</u>. This stands for <u>"before anyone else"</u>, and thus is used to describe your significant other, or perhaps, if you are single, your pet, or even a bottle of cranberry juice as I noted yesterday. I really cannot refresh Twitter fast enough to keep up with all the baes flying around cyberspace.

Of course, language evolves, and as a word-lover I'm all for that, but it seems to be evolving in the wrong direction. Now, when people write online they use a horrible pseudo-emotional language instead of expressing themselves coherently. As someone who meticulously spells out every word of a text or tweet (although I do allow myself an ironic "lolz" occasionally) I am aware that I may sound like an ancient stick-in-the-mud. But because I write for a living, I hate to see language butchered like this.

Take for instance <u>"I can't even"</u>. It's basically someone saying they can't comprehend something and thus cannot express themselves. Perhaps someone got their coffee order wrong. Or they saw a hilarious <u>Ryan Gosling Vine</u>. But it makes me want to shout "You can't even WHAT???"

And then there's the utterly loathsome <u>"all the feels"</u>. This is used to signify that the user is having a strong emotion, or perhaps several emotions at once. Maybe they accidentally <u>swiped left</u> on Tinder, or they've seen a picture of a dog wearing a hat, or bae hasn't texted them back. This is troubling, because if you are feeling emotional, the internet really isn't the place for you. Go and talk to a real person about how that hat-wearing dog makes you feel, for goodness sake.

This mode of expression is breeding a generation that is doing two problematic things simultaneously: having overblown emotional responses to commonplace events, while also being utterly unable to express appropriate and coherent emotions.

So, young people of the internet, what I have to say to you in 2015 is: <u>can you not</u>?

Twerking, selfie and unlike? Young people don't speak like that – I should know

It doesn't exactly reflect well on young people that the new additions to the Oxford Dictionaries Online are mostly related to image, reputation and sex, writes 20 year-old Isabelle Kerr, who questions why these slang words have been elevated to a level of permanence and authority.

By Isabelle Kerr

4:10PM BST 28 Aug 2013

I'm so gonna unlike that selfie of her twerking. Srsly though, these words make me wanna vom.

If you were to look in the most recent catalogue of the Oxford Dictionary of the English Language online you would think something appalling had happened. Among some of the greatest and most eloquent words in the English language, an invasion of bizarre, nonsensical and downright pointless words appear to have taken over.

The Oxford Dictionaries Online have announced plans to include a variety of new, shall we say, colloquial words to their online collection, including slang words such as vom, selfie, unlike, digital detox, food baby and more. Sadly these are not misprints, nor has Word accidentally changed misspelt words into a seemingly-foreign language. These are in fact the pitiful emblems of the current young generation's contribution to language. My generation. I am 20.

Among the new additions, 'twerking' has taken centre stage. I actually had to Google this word yesterday when investigating why Miley Cyrus was said to have 'twerked' at the MTV video music awards.

The official definition reads: "Twerk, v.: dance to popular music in a sexually provocative manner involving thrusting hip movements and a low, squatting stance." Right.

As a member of the younger generation, partly responsible for these linguistic calamities, I can only apologise. I am embarrassed and ashamed. It doesn't exactly reflect well on young people that the new additions are mostly related to image, reputation and sex. Instead of creating words to improve our ability to communicate and express ourselves, these words simply promulgate an unhealthy culture obsessed with being seen in the right places and knowing who's doing what.

It's already a constant battle for young people to prove we're not all apathetic, ASBO-wielding yobs who can't communicate properly. These recent additions to the dictionary certainly do us no favours. Comments on Twitter and online today have enhanced our image problem. One online user wrote "no wonder there is so much youth unemployment"; whilst another tweeted "it's over. They've won".

ANSWERS

Practice Exam 1

English Language

Paper 1: Language, the Individual and Society

Section A: Textual Variations and Representations

1.	Analyse how **Text A** uses language to create meanings and representations.	**[25 marks]**
	This question is marked out of 10 for AO1 and out of 15 for AO3. Both AOs should be consistently addressed throughout your answer so there will be overlap between them.	
	Use these grids to focus on your level for each skill.	

AO1: Apply appropriate methods of language analysis, using associated terminology and coherent written expression.

Level marks	At this level	Indicative content
Level 5 9–10	**Students will:** • **apply linguistic methods and terminology, identifying patterns and complexities** • **apply different levels of language analysis in an integrated way, recognising how they are connected** • **apply levels of language analysis with rare errors** • **guide the reader.**	Text A uses field-specific lexis such as 'antibiotic' and 'immune system' sparingly in order to support the broadly formal discourse pattern. The use of medical terminology demonstrates that the source is reliable and trustworthy, while the avoidance of overuse or straying into exclusionary jargon territory allows it to maintain its publicly accessible format. Text A's use of modal auxiliary verbs 'can' and 'shouldn't' demonstrates the levels of certainty that it needs to present to patients. The text has to tread a fine line between being accessible and authoritative, which is achieved by the use of modals that express a high degree of certainty/obligation but are not absolute.
Level 4 7–8	**Students will:** • **apply linguistic methods and terminology with precision and detail** • **apply two or more levels of language analysis** • **apply levels of language analysis with occasional errors** • **develop a line of argument.**	Text A uses both lexis and discourse to represent its meaning and convey its information. It employs field-specific lexis 'immune system' to create a formal tone and supports this with clear, imperative sentence structures. It also uses bullet points and subheadings to present information in a clear, direct manner that is in keeping with the overall formality that is needed to maintain a level of authority.
Level 3 5–6	**Students will:** • **apply linguistic methods and terminology consistently and appropriately** • **label features that have value for the task** • **label features with more accuracy than inaccuracy** • **communicate with clear topics and paragraphs.**	Text A uses direct address with the pronoun 'you' in order to make sure that the reader knows who is being spoken about and feels like they are being involved in the text. There is also technical lexis such as 'antiseptic', 'antibiotics' and 'immune system', which shows that the semantic field of healthcare and medicine is being used.
Level 2 3–4	**Students will:** • **use linguistic methods and terminology inconsistently and sometimes without value for the task** • **generalise about language use with limited/unclear evidence** • **label features with more inaccuracy than accuracy** • **express ideas with organisation emerging.**	Text A uses the pronoun 'you' to talk to the reader. This is because it needs to sound like it has authority, so it says things about the reader. There are also lots of different verbs used to create sentence structures.
Level 1 1–2	**Students will:** • **quote or identify features of language without linguistic description** • **present material with limited organisation.**	Text A uses bullet points to show different things people can do to cure a sore throat. There are lots of examples of things to do, including going to the GP or calling 999. There is some repetition of bullet points such as 'use' and 'you'.

AO3: Analyse and evaluate how contextual factors and language features are associated with the construction of meaning.		
Level marks	**At this level**	**Indicative content**
Level 5 13–15	**Students will:** • **evaluate use of language and representations according to context** • **explore analysis within wider social and cultural contexts.**	The text is an online piece, which means it is more likely to be accessed by younger adults who are adept at using technology for a variety of purposes and navigating large websites such as the NHS Choices site. The text takes an authoritative tone with a high number of imperative constructions throughout, which is consistent with the purpose of giving medical advice from a trusted source. It is also linked to the unstated purpose of the website, which is to keep non-serious illnesses from being brought to GPs or A&E and therefore lessen the burden on the NHS. The text is likely to be trusted, as the NHS is seen as a reliable institution and one whose health advice is relevant, accurate and up to date. This is also supported by references to other NHS services such as GPs and calling 999 or 111. At no point is the writer referenced through any means – no use of personal pronouns – this creates distance between reader and writer. The text goes some way towards countering this by using some less formal lexis: 'nothing to worry about', 'although there's little proof they help'.
Level 4 10–12	**Students will:** • **analyse how language choices create meanings and representations** • **analyse how aspects of context work together to affect language use.**	Text A's consistent use of imperative constructions to issue instructions on healthcare is consistent with its implied status, coming from the NHS – a reputable and reliable source of healthcare information. The text creates a significant distance between reader and writer, this is partly due to the online, non-interactive nature of the text and partly due to the necessity to maintain a sense of professional formality and distance. There is evidence, however, of the writer attempting to counteract this distance – presumably as it could be seen as off-putting for readers – by using informal constructions such as 'nothing to worry about' that create a more informal tone right at the start of the text. This is linked to the purpose of the text; to reassure people about what is 'normally' a very minor ailment.
Level 3 7–9	**Students will:** • **interpret significance of specific choices of language according to context** • **link specific language choices with an aspect of context.**	Text A uses two sentence types consistently – declaratives and imperatives. It is appropriate to use imperatives because the text is giving instructions on how to cure a sore throat. This shows that the writer of the text is knowledgeable and expects to be trusted by the reader. The NHS is a trusted authority on health issues in the UK, so the writer can reasonably expect to be taken seriously.
Level 2 4–6	**Students will:** • **identify distinctive features of language and significant aspects of context.**	Text A gives people instructions on how to cure a sore throat and what to do if it doesn't get better. It is from the NHS website, so people will trust what it says. The information is broken down into bullet points to make it easy to follow – each bullet point gives a new instruction to help cure the shore throat. It also goes through different things to do if the last thing didn't work: see pharmacist, visit GP, call 999.
Level 1 1–3	**Students will:** • **paraphrase or describe content of texts** • **misunderstand text or context.**	Text A is about curing a sore throat and giving advice on how to do this. It tells you what to do and when you should go to the GP for medicine. Everyone would see this text as it is online.

2.	Analyse how **Text B** uses language to create meanings and representations. **[25 marks]**
	This question is marked out of 10 for AO1 and out of 15 for AO3. Both AOs should be consistently addressed throughout your answer so there will be overlap between them.
	Use these grids to focus on your level for each skill:

AO1: Apply appropriate methods of language analysis, using associated terminology and coherent written expression.

Level marks	At this level	Indicative content
Level 5 9–10	Students will: • **apply linguistic methods and terminology, identifying patterns and complexities** • **apply different levels of language analysis in an integrated way, recognising how they are connected** • **apply levels of language analysis with rare errors** • **guide the reader.**	Text B's title 'Female Recipe Book' leads a modern reader to expect recipes for food. This, however, is not the case, which suggests that the word 'recipe' has undergone semantic shift in the past 200 years and that in 1818 it had a medical application to its meaning. There are elements that suggest there is a core of similarity to the meaning of this lexis as Text B does contain a list of ingredients and instructions: 'drink a table spoonful of warm milk, with a great deal of pepper in it, wash it down with warm milk', but they are not in a format we would anticipate in the twenty-first century.
Level 4 7–8	Students will: • **apply linguistic methods and terminology with precision and detail** • **apply two or more levels of language analysis** • **apply levels of language analysis with occasional errors** • **develop a line of argument.**	The use of the word 'recipe' in the title of Text B suggests that lexical change has happened in the 200 years since the book's publication as it does not conform to our modern expectations of what a recipe would look like or the way it would be structured. The word 'recipe' seems to have either changed or narrowed its meaning in context as we would no longer expect to see it in use in a medical context.
Level 3 5–6	Students will: • **apply linguistic methods and terminology consistently and appropriately** • **label features that have value for the task** • **label features with more accuracy than inaccuracy** • **communicate with clear topics and paragraphs.**	Text B uses the word 'recipe' in the title but does not seem to contain any recipes in the modern sense of the word. This may be because the lexis has changed in the past 200 years. There is some evidence of a recipe for a cure for lumps in the throat that includes instructions for how to make and use it but it does not provide specific quantities or methods.
Level 2 3–4	Students will: • **use linguistic methods and terminology inconsistently and sometimes without value for the task** • **generalise about language use with limited/unclear evidence** • **label features with more inaccuracy than accuracy** • **express ideas with organisation emerging.**	Text B is called a 'Female Recipe Book' and it gives some instructions for making a range of cures for different types of sore throat but it doesn't present them as recipes like we would expect them today.
Level 1 1–2	Students will: • **quote or identify features of language without linguistic description** • **present material with limited organisation.**	Text B uses the word 'recipe' in its title and gives some ideas for recipes to make medicines to cure throat problems.

AO3: Analyse and evaluate how contextual factors and language features are associated with the construction of meaning.

Level marks	At this level	Indicative content
Level 5 13–15	Students will: • **evaluate use of language and representations according to context** • **explore analysis within wider social and cultural contexts.**	Text B was written in 1818 and has a very clearly defined audience of women, which is stated in the title 'female recipe book'. The areas with which the book concerns itself – childcare and home healthcare – are traditionally female spheres and therefore the book is targeted specifically at them. It does not, however, talk down to the reader. Instead it assumes a reasonable degree of understanding about anatomy, medicine and healthcare, evidenced by its lack of supporting explanation for a number of technical terms such as 'glands', 'scurvy' and 'tumour'.
Level 4 10–12	Students will: • **analyse how language choices create meanings and representations** • **analyse how aspects of context work together to affect language use.**	Text B presents itself as authoritative and gives instructional advice on how to treat 'lumps in the throat or glands'. It uses medical terminology in context and refers to treatments that were in common use in 1818 such as 'leeches', 'Ether's mineral' and 'spirits of hartsthorn'. The text is aimed at women who were able to read complex texts, so this would limit the audience to the middle classes and above, which is supported by the expectations of readers' knowledge and understanding of the ingredients and treatments described.
Level 3 7–9	Students will: • **interpret significance of specific choices of language according to context** • **link specific language choices with an aspect of context.**	Text B was written in 1818 and gives advice to women on how to deal with aspects of childcare and healthcare. It uses the language of healthcare that was available at the time and makes reference to medicines: 'Epsom salts', treatments: 'bathe the lumps with strong salt and water' and escalating severity of illness: 'seek professional skill'. All of these references are expected to be understood by the reader, as no further explanation is offered as to what they are or how to carry them out.
Level 2 4–6	Students will: • **identify distinctive features of language and significant aspects of context.**	Text B was published in 1818 and is aimed at showing women how to do things such as childcare and healthcare. The text gives different possible causes of 'lumps in the throat or glands' and instructions on how to treat the different possibilities. The text relies on medicinal treatments that were common in 1818, so the variety of treatments includes 'leeches' and wearing a piece of 'root round the stomach'.
Level 1 1–3	Students will: • **paraphrase or describe content of texts** • **misunderstand text or context.**	Text B is a 200-year-old book giving advice on how to treat a sore throat. The book is aimed at women because it is called a 'female recipe book'. The book gives different ways to cure 'lumps in the throat or glands'.

3.	Explore the similarities and differences in the ways **Text A** and **Text B** use language. **This question is marked out of 20 for AO4.**	[20 marks]

AO4: Explore connections across texts, informed by linguistic concepts and methods.

Level marks	At this level	Indicative content
Level 5 17–20	Students will: • **evaluate the importance/significance/effect of connections found across texts.**	Both texts take a clear, authoritative tone that makes use of mostly declarative and imperative sentence structures in order to convey information and give instructions on treating medical conditions. While they both deal with audiences who have the literacy levels to access their information, the changing nature of healthcare in the 200 years that divides them means that Text A, coming from the official NHS website, is produced in line with public health guidelines and as part of a multifaceted healthcare system that was not relevant in the older text. This means that Text A will have been scrupulously checked before publication and will be part of a rolling programme of updates, unlike Text B, and must therefore be particularly clear and careful to mitigate against any possible misinterpretations. This necessity for accuracy is not present in Text B as can be seen by the lack of specific guidance on quantity or frequency of use of the cures it describes. This points to a significant difference in the texts' relationships with their audiences and suggests a direct correlation between accountability and the degree of detail included in such a text.
Level 4 13–16	Students will: • **explore connections between texts by linking language and context.**	Texts A and B both use a combination of declarative and imperative sentence structures to give instructions and advice to people who want to treat a sore throat. They both start off at the simplest, most innocuous type of sore throat and advise a simple treatment range. Both texts then go through a series of steps that escalate what to do if the problem doesn't go away or becomes worse. In Text A this sequence is a very formalised process through NHS systems from pharmacist to GP to calling 999, whereas in Text B there is a suggestion for a more radical treatment followed by an instruction to consult a chemist and then to 'seek professional skill' if none of the previous options has been successful. This shows a similar approach to treatment despite the different methods of delivery.
Level 3 9–12	Students will: • **make connections across texts by identifying similar or different uses of language/content/context.**	Texts A and B both use lots of instructions and imperative sentences to tell the reader what to do to treat a sore throat. They also both use a mixture of technical language such as 'symptoms' and 'scurvy' and less formal words in order to make sure the reader trusts them but can still understand them.
Level 2 5–8	Students will: • **make connections at a literal level.**	Both Text A and B are about how to treat a sore throat. They give different advice because they were written at different times. Both texts tell you how to use medicines or home remedies to treat the problem and also what to do if it gets worse.
Level 1 1–4	Students will: • **discuss relevant aspects of texts without making connections explicitly.**	Text A is about how the NHS treats sore throats and what to do about it if they do not get better. It is aimed at people who want reassurance about their illness and also who know about the website. Text B is about how 'lumps in the throat or glands' were treated in 1818. In those days it was mostly women who cared for people so the book it aimed at them.

Section B: Child Language Development

4.	'More Knowledgeable Others play a major part in child language development.' Referring to Data Set 1 in detail, and to relevant ideas from language study, evaluate this view of children's language development. **[30 marks]** **This question is marked out of 15 for AO1 and out of 15 for AO2. Both AOs should be consistently addressed throughout your answer so there will be overlap between them.** **Use these grids to focus on your level for each skill:**

AO1: Apply appropriate methods of language analysis, using associated terminology and coherent written expression.

Level marks	At this level	Indicative content
Level 5 13–15	Students will: • **apply linguistic methods and terminology, identifying patterns and complexities** • **apply different levels of language analysis in an integrated way, recognising how they are connected** • **apply levels of language analysis with rare errors** • **guide the reader.**	Lizzy uses temporal language in sentences with grammatical accuracy; she clearly understands which lexis falls into this category and how to differentiate between 'days of the week' and 'yesterday/today/tomorrow'. Her accuracy rate is variable in her use of the terms, however, which brings to mind Piaget's research on cognitive understanding of a concept and Lizzy's ability to apply this knowledge. She may not yet be completely confident about the different relationships between days of the week and 'yesterday/today/tomorrow' so is still developing her accuracy in using the language surrounding them.
Level 4 10–12	Students will: • **apply linguistic methods and terminology with precision and detail** • **apply two or more levels of language analysis** • **apply levels of language analysis with occasional errors** • **develop a line of argument.**	Jessica, Lizzy and their mother all use a range of temporal language to frame the discussion about Lizzy being 'special helper' at pre-school. Jessica's use of lexis relating to time is almost completely fluent, with her only minor lapses being in grammatical construction rather than comprehension of timeframes. Lizzy demonstrates a wide range of time-related vocabulary from days of the week: 'Sunday', to the vocabulary required to discuss their relationship to one another: 'today', 'yesterday'. This is clearly an area that Lizzy is motivated to use, which may be because she understands its importance in communicating meaning with accuracy. Lizzy's willingness to copy and be corrected by Jessica supports Vygotsky's assertion that siblings can be MKOs and support one another's language development.
Level 3 7–9	Students will: • **apply linguistic methods and terminology consistently and appropriately** • **label features that have value for the task** • **label features with more accuracy than inaccuracy** • **communicate with clear topics and paragraphs.**	Lizzy uses language related to time with varying degrees of accuracy. It is clearly something that she is trying to understand and use to make herself understood. Jessica has mastered this structure and corrects some of Lizzy's statements: 'tomorrow, you mean Monday' which shows that Jessica understands both what Lizzy was trying to say and how it relates to the time frame they are discussing (as they presumably won't be at nursery on Saturday). Lizzy is able and willing to copy her older sister's utterances: 'can't do it yet', which supports Skinner's behaviourist theory.
Level 2 4–6	Students will: • **use linguistic methods and terminology inconsistently and sometimes without value for the task** • **generalise about language use with limited/unclear evidence** • **label features with more inaccuracy than accuracy** • **express ideas with organisation emerging.**	Lizzy talks about what she has done today and what she will do on other days by using words such as 'yesterday', 'Monday', 'Sunday' and asking questions like 'what day is it today?' This shows she understands about days of the week. She copies her sister because of the behaviourist theory by Skinner.
Level 1 1–3	Students will: • **quote or identify features of language without linguistic description** • **present material with limited organisation.**	Lizzy uses words and phrases to refer to time and days of the week, but she does not seem to know how these fit together. She copies her older sister when she corrects her.

AO2: Demonstrate critical understanding of concepts and issues relevant to language use.		
Level marks	At this level	Indicative content
Level 5 13–15	Students will: • demonstrate a synthesised, conceptualised and individual overview of issues • evaluate and challenge views, approaches and interpretations of linguistic issues.	As she is two years older, Jessica functions as a More Knowledgeable Other (MKO) when speaking with Lizzy; the two girls use adjacency pairs as part of their turn-taking structure with Jessica's utterances being almost completely grammatically accurate whilst Lizzy's are developing and currently around the post-telegraphic stage with typical features such as pronoun omission in evidence: 'Mummy can't do it'. The fact that Lizzy repeats Jessica's pronunciation of 'can't' in the standard format using the /k/ shows that she has been strongly influenced by her sister as an MKO.
Level 4 10–12	Students will: • identify and comment on different views, approaches and interpretations of linguistic issues.	Jessica's status as a More Knowledgeable Other for Lizzy is shown when she models a standard pronunciation of 'can't' back to Lizzy and Lizzy repeats it with accuracy even though in her first attempt at the utterance she substituted the /k/ with /t/ as it is an easier sound. Lizzy seems to respond more to Jessica's utterances than to her mother's – possibly because Jessica is actively correcting whereas the mother is not.
Level 3 7–9	Students will: • show detailed knowledge of linguistic ideas, concepts and research.	Jessica has a role as a More Knowledgeable Other for Lizzy as her language is significantly more developed. This can be seen in her high level of grammatical accuracy and ability to self-correct: 'were you in, were you the', as opposed to Lizzy's language, which appears to be at the post-telegraphic stage.
Level 2 4–6	Students will: • show familiarity with linguistic ideas, concepts and research.	Both Jessica and Lizzy use More Knowledgeable Others. This can be seen when they interrupt each other. Jessica's sentences are better than Lizzy's because she is older and knows more words.
Level 1 1–3	Students will: • discuss issues anecdotally without specialist linguistic knowledge.	Jessica corrects Lizzy because she is older and better at using language.

5.	'Children prefer to focus on the content of their writing rather than accurate spelling.' Referring to Data Set 2 and Data Set 3 in detail, and to relevant ideas from language study, evaluate this view of children's language development. **[30 marks]** **This question is marked out of 15 for AO1 and out of 15 for AO2. Both AOs should be consistently addressed throughout your answer so there will be overlap between them.** **Use these grids to focus on your level for each skill:**

AO1: Apply appropriate methods of language analysis, using associated terminology and coherent written expression.

Level marks	At this level	Indicative Content
Level 5 13–15	Students will: • **apply linguistic methods and terminology, identifying patterns and complexities** • **apply different levels of language analysis in an integrated way, recognising how they are connected** • **apply levels of language analysis with rare errors** • **guide the reader.**	Jessica uses her phonetic understanding of language to inform her writing. She extends the 'wh' at the start of 'when' to the start of 'whent' later in the sentence and across the two texts shows variation in her spellings of 'was' as 'wos' and 'waz', which suggest that she is familiar with some elements of the spelling but has not yet put them together. Chomsky might describe these phoneme–grapheme links and variations as virtuous errors as they can be seen to attempt to conform with orthographic standards, disproving the question's assertion regarding children's preferred focus when writing. Jessica has written both of these texts at home and has chosen topics in her own personal experience as her subject matter. Her parents have given her support with some spellings but clearly not all as her accuracy is still developing. Interestingly, the only mirrored letter she has used (the 's' in Christmas) is in one of the words that she asked for support with.
Level 4 10–12	Students will: • **apply linguistic methods and terminology with precision and detail** • **apply two or more levels of language analysis** • **apply levels of language analysis with occasional errors** • **develop a line of argument.**	Jessica's orthography is heavily influenced by phoneme–grapheme links as can be seen in words such as 'lunden' and 'gowin'. Each of these is a reasonable phonetic representation of the word and shows that Jessica has a grasp of the connections between the two. It appears that Jessica is in the consolidation stage of her written development according to Kroll, as she is crafting logical grammatical constructions that sometimes mimic speech as in the 'and' construction in the Christmas text but can also represent written sentence styles.
Level 3 7–9	Students will: • **apply linguistic methods and terminology consistently and appropriately** • **label features that have value for the task** • **label features with more accuracy than inaccuracy** • **communicate with clear topics and paragraphs.**	Jessica's orthography is developing, and she shows that she is able to make links between phoneme and grapheme, though these links can give varied results. She clearly requests support from adults with some longer words and reproduces these with accurate orthography but some lapses in stylistics such as the lower case 'c' and mirrored 's'. The topics of both texts are personal and show that Jessica enjoys writing about her experiences, which supports the statement in the question. The fact that she asks for help shows that Skinner's behaviourist theory is right as she wants the praise for being correct.
Level 2 4–6	Students will: • **use linguistic methods and terminology inconsistently and sometimes without value for the task** • **generalise about language use with limited/unclear evidence** • **label features with more inaccuracy than accuracy** • **express ideas with organisation emerging.**	Some of Jessica's lexis is accurate and shows that she is writing about events that happened to her personally. She is able to use correct spellings when she has support from an adult. Asking an adult is supporting Vygotsky's ideas about MKOs. Jessica's written language is developing and shows that she sounds out her spellings.
Level 1 1–3	Students will: • **quote or identify features of language without linguistic description** • **present material with limited organisation.**	Jessica uses a range of features that have a mixture of accuracy. The words that she has had support with are spelled correctly, such as 'Christmas' and 'nativity'. This shows that adults are important when children learn language like in Skinner's theory.

AO2: Demonstrate critical understanding of concepts and issues relevant to language use.		
Level marks	At this level	Indicative content
Level 5 13–15	Students will: • **demonstrate a synthesised, conceptualised and individual overview of issues** • **evaluate and challenge views, approaches and interpretations of linguistic issues.**	When children begin to learn to write they will typically be encouraged to put their ideas down on paper and not to be overly concerned with orthography outside of formal school lessons, as it would be unrealistic to expect a child to spell all words accurately as soon as they begin to write. As Jessica has written these texts at home she is unlikely to have been particularly concerned with spelling as she is writing, because she wants to share her experiences. She does, however, display a level of concern for technical accuracy when she seeks support with polysyllabic lexis such as 'nativity' and 'Christmas' – the longest words she writes in these texts. This suggests that whilst the representations function (Halliday) is her primary focus, she also wants to ensure that she can be understood.
Level 4 10–12	Students will: • **identify and comment on different views, approaches and interpretations of linguistic issues.**	Jessica uses Halliday's representational function to write about her experiences in London and in the nativity play. Throughout her writing she uses both standard and non-standard orthography, seeking support with more complex vocabulary. She knows that her parents are More Knowledgeable Others and therefore seeks support from them when she feels it is necessary. At other times she is happy to use her own skills to construct the texts, which results in some lapses in accuracy as she develops her understanding of English spelling systems.
Level 3 7–9	Students will: • **show detailed knowledge of linguistic ideas, concepts and research.**	Jessica's texts both fall into the category of representational function as identified by Halliday. She is recounting events she has participated in that she has found interesting or exciting so her primary purpose is to get her ideas across, rather than to ensure accurate orthography throughout. Jessica does have some concern for accuracy though as she has sought support from her parents in order to spell some words correctly, such as 'nativity'.
Level 2 4–6	Students will: • **show familiarity with linguistic ideas, concepts and research.**	Jessica did ask her parents for support with some of her spellings, which shows that she does want to get them right, but she does not seek support for all of them, so she is happy to make her own phoneme–grapheme links in order to complete her writing about her experiences.
Level 1 1–3	Students will: • **discuss issues anecdotally without specialist linguistic knowledge.**	Jessica makes a range of accuracy lapses in her writing, which shows that she does not mind about spellings as long as she gets her point across.

Practice Exam 1

English Language

Paper 2: Language, Diversity and Change

Section A: Diversity and Change

1.	Evaluate the idea that powerful people use powerful language	[30 marks]
	This question is marked out of 10 for AO1 and out of 20 for AO2. Both AOs should be consistently addressed throughout your answer so there will be overlap between them.	
	Use these grids to focus on your level for each skill.	

AO1: Apply appropriate methods of language analysis, using associated terminology and coherent written expression.

Level marks	At this level
Level 5 9–10	Students will: • apply linguistic methods and terminology, identifying patterns and complexities • apply different levels of language analysis in an integrated way, recognising how they are connected • apply levels of language analysis with rare errors • guide the reader.
Level 4 7–8	Students will: • apply linguistic methods and terminology with precision and detail • apply two or more levels of language analysis • apply levels of language analysis with occasional errors • develop a line of argument.
Level 3 5–6	Students will: • apply linguistic methods and terminology consistently and appropriately • label features that have value for the task • label features with more accuracy than inaccuracy • communicate with clear topics and paragraphs.
Level 2 3–4	Students will: • use linguistic methods and terminology inconsistently and sometimes without value for the task • generalise about language use with limited/unclear evidence • label features with more inaccuracy than accuracy • express ideas with organisation emerging.
Level 1 1–2	Students will: • quote or identify features of language without linguistic description • present material with limited organisation.

AO2: Demonstrate critical understanding of concepts and issues relevant to language use.	
Level marks	At this level
Level 5 17–20	Students will: • demonstrate a synthesised, conceptualised and individual overview of issues • evaluate and challenge views, approaches and interpretations of linguistic issues.
Level 4 13–16	Students will: • identify and comment on different views, approaches and interpretations of linguistic issues.
Level 3 9–12	Students will: • show detailed knowledge of linguistic ideas, concepts and research.
Level 2 5–8	Students will: • show familiarity with linguistic ideas, concepts and research.
Level 1 1–4	Students will: • discuss issues anecdotally without specialist linguistic knowledge.

There are many possible responses to this question. Here is an example part of a possible answer:

What constitutes powerful language? There is no small amount of debate among linguists themselves, so in order to evaluate whether powerful people use powerful language it must be understood what is meant by each term. There are three different types of power identified by Wareing, which are: political power, personal power and social group power. Different people will be powerful in different situations and for different reasons. It is therefore true that different types of language would be considered powerful in different contexts – what is powerful when being spoken by a police officer when questioning a suspect would be entirely inappropriate for a social situation and would therefore not be socially powerful. I will also need to evaluate whether language is considered powerful because it is being used by powerful people or whether the language used by powerful people is inherently powerful in and of itself. Powerful people wield their power in ways that go beyond the language they use, but the ability to use words to meet their goals is an integral part of success.

This partial answer makes relevant reference to language theories and sets out a clear trajectory for addressing the issues raised in the set task.

AO1: A line of enquiry is clearly set out and demonstrates an understanding of the different language levels that must be discussed in order to address the question.

AO2: This partial response shows a clear understanding of what the question is asking by immediately referencing Wareing's three types of power. This sets up a response that can look at different perspectives on power and how a range of theories could be referred to. The ideas laid out in this opening paragraph, if completed in full, would suggest a response at Level 4.

2.	Evaluate the idea that language change is beyond prescriptive jurisdiction. [30 marks]
	This question is marked out of 10 for AO1 and out of 20 for AO2. Both AOs should be consistently addressed throughout your answer so there will be overlap between them.
	Use these grids to focus on your level for each skill.

AO1: Apply appropriate methods of language analysis, using associated terminology and coherent written expression.

Level marks	At this level
Level 5 9–10	Students will: • apply linguistic methods and terminology, identifying patterns and complexities • apply different levels of language analysis in an integrated way, recognising how they are connected • apply levels of language analysis with rare errors • guide the reader.
Level 4 7–8	Students will: • apply linguistic methods and terminology with precision and detail • apply two or more levels of language analysis • apply levels of language analysis with occasional errors • develop a line of argument.
Level 3 5–6	Students will: • apply linguistic methods and terminology consistently and appropriately • label features that have value for the task • label features with more accuracy than inaccuracy • communicate with clear topics and paragraphs.
Level 2 3–4	Students will: • use linguistic methods and terminology inconsistently and sometimes without value for the task • generalise about language use with limited/unclear evidence • label features with more inaccuracy than accuracy • express ideas with organisation emerging.
Level 1 1–2	Students will: • quote or identify features of language without linguistic description • present material with limited organisation.

AO2: Demonstrate critical understanding of concepts and issues relevant to language use.	
Level marks	At this level
Level 5 17–20	**Students will:** • demonstrate a synthesised, conceptualised and individual overview of issues • evaluate and challenge views, approaches and interpretations of linguistic issues.
Level 4 13–16	**Students will:** • identify and comment on different views, approaches and interpretations of linguistic issues.
Level 3 9–12	**Students will:** • show detailed knowledge of linguistic ideas, concepts and research.
Level 2 5–8	**Students will:** • show familiarity with linguistic ideas, concepts and research.
Level 1 1–4	**Students will:** • discuss issues anecdotally without specialist linguistic knowledge.

There are many possible responses to this question. Here is an example part of a possible answer:

Language change is an inevitable part of the life of any language as a language must have living speakers to be considered truly alive itself. These speakers will innovate, alter and create new content for the language, as can be seen by looking at texts from different time periods for any number of different languages. Perhaps the only way in which a language can avoid change is for it to 'die' – as a 'dead' language, albeit one that is still in regular use for scholarly purposes, Latin undergoes minimal if any change, mostly because it has no native speakers. The English language, on the other hand, changes at a rate so swift that even lexicographers will admit that their dictionaries are immediately out of date upon publication. Samuel Johnson, who published the first commonly accepted English Dictionary in 1755 changed his view during his own writing process from initially wishing to preserve and create a correct form of English, to admitting that this goal was an impossible one and accepting that his role was more descriptive than prescriptive, and preeminent linguist David Crystal maintains that language is 'never static'.

This opening paragraph demonstrates a clear grasp of the question and an understanding of the concepts and issues that are relevant to exploring the topic.

AO1: Linguistic terminology is appropriately selected and accurately applied. This introduction could be strengthened by making explicit reference to the different language levels it will be necessary to analyse in order to provide a robust response. A line of argument is clearly set out.

AO2: This introduction clearly demonstrates a conceptualised overview of language change as a topic, showing an understanding of the changing nature of living languages and making a robust and detailed reference to the prescriptive attitudes mentioned in the question. A response that continued at this level would have a strong AO2 leading a weaker AO1 and could achieve a mark around a low Level 4.

Section B: Language Discourses

3.	Analyse how language is used in Text A and Text B to present ideas about gendered language. In your answer you should:

• examine any similarities and differences you find between the texts
• explore how effectively the texts present their views. **[40 marks]**

This question is marked out of 10 for AO1, out of 15 for AO3 and out of 15 for AO4. All AOs should be consistently addressed throughout your answer so there will be overlap between them.

Use these grids to focus on your level for each skill.

AO1: Apply appropriate methods of language analysis, using associated terminology and coherent written expression.

Level marks	At this level	Indicative content
Level 5 9–10	Students will: • apply linguistic methods and terminology, identifying patterns and complexities • apply different levels of language analysis in an integrated way, recognising how they are connected • apply levels of language analysis with rare errors • guide the reader.	Text B uses Latinate lexis: 'admonished', and passive constructions: 'has been partially blamed for the pay gap' to suggest its disagreement with the phenomenon it describes. These techniques show that the writer wishes to distance herself from the research on which she is reporting and this demonstrates a clear degree of disdain for the problems that it highlights. The opening line: 'Children as young as five are going to be admonished…' focuses on the very youngest children in primary school and contrasts this with overly formal, almost archaic lexis ('admonished') in order to present the topic as a disproportionate response to a minor problem. This is in contrast to Text A which, whilst taking a less formal tone, clearly feels that it is making 'an important point'. The contrasting tones of the articles and their differing views on the subject matter appear to be contrary to what readers might expect; the more formal, serious Text B taking the less serious view and Text A using a humorously large number of portmanteau neologisms: 'manspreading', 'girlboss' to support genuine concerns about how the language we use shapes the way we think about different topics.
Level 4 7–8	Students will: • apply linguistic methods and terminology with precision and detail • apply two or more levels of language analysis • apply levels of language analysis with occasional errors • develop a line of argument.	The tone of Text A is fairly informal and lighthearted. This can be seen through the lexical choices and in the discourse of the article. Mahdawi uses neologisms such as 'mansplain', 'guyliner' and 'mumtrepreneur', all of which are portmanteau words and therefore sound a little jarring in their mashing together of existing terms to make new ones; this links to the generally informal tone of the article, which uses discourse markers such as rhetorical questions in order to make clear the assumption that the reader agrees with the writer's point of view.
Level 3 5–6	Students will: • apply linguistic methods and terminology consistently and appropriately • label features that have value for the task • label features with more accuracy than inaccuracy • communicate with clear topics and paragraphs.	Text A starts presenting the argument with a degree of humour as the large number of portmanteau words such as 'mansplain', 'guyliner' and 'mumtrepreneur', which the writer uses as examples, are mostly new entries to the language and many carry little formality. Text B focuses on the use of insults in a school context, so the lexis the writer focuses on is more in terms of how it could deepen the divide between girls and boys at school.

Level 2 3–4	Students will: • **use linguistic methods and terminology inconsistently and sometimes without value for the task** • **generalise about language use with limited/unclear evidence** • **label features with more inaccuracy than accuracy** • **express ideas with organisation emerging.**	Text A focuses on new words and new mixed words such as 'guyliner' and how they are used to refer to one gender and not the other. Text B talks about how different insults are used in schools and how these are linked to being a girl or a boy. Most of the words and phrases are suggesting that girls are not as good as boys.
Level 1 1–2	Students will: • **quote or identify features of language without linguistic description** • **present material with limited organisation.**	Both texts are about gendered language. They both use lots of examples of the kinds of language they are talking about such as 'girlboss' and 'man up'. Text A talks about how the words are not really equal. Text B talks about why different words are being used at school.

AO3: Analyse and evaluate how contextual factors and language features are associated with the construction of meaning.		
Level marks	At this level	Indicative content
Level 5 13–15	**Students will:** • **evaluate use of language and representations according to context** • **explore analysis within wider social and cultural contexts.**	Readership of online newspaper websites is largely self-selecting, though the Guardian is not behind a paywall so this could bring a broader audience to some articles. It is a broadly liberal publication and the nature of online journalism means that readers will have chosen to view this article by clicking through to find it based on a headline and perhaps an image or subheading. This means that the writer can assume a basic level of agreement from the majority of her readers and therefore will not need to explain the neologisms ('feminazi') or cultural references ('Netflix') she is making. The writer assumes that her readers will be broadly in agreement with the social values of the publication and can therefore afford to employ the less formal tone without risking the topic being dismissed as unimportant.
Level 4 10–12	**Students will:** • **analyse how language choices create meanings and representations** • **analyse how aspects of context work together to affect language use.**	Text A is taken from the Guardian website, which means that the expected readership is self-selecting. Readers will have had to click through at least one page to reach the article so they will already have expressed a degree of interest in the topic by doing so. This means that the writer can assume that they are likeminded at least to a basic degree and does not need to explain in detail any of the portmanteau neologisms she uses to exemplify the problem she perceives in their use.
Level 3 7–9	**Students will:** • **interpret significance of specific choices of language according to context** • **link specific language choices with an aspect of context.**	Text A is taken from the Guardian website so the people reading it will be likely to mainly agree with the newspaper's opinions on different issues. This means the language used will be more towards an educated, young adult or liberal viewpoint and that there will be no need to explain what hashtags and Netflix are as it is assumed knowledge.
Level 2 4–6	**Students will:** • **identify distinctive features of language and significant aspects of context.**	Text A appears on the Guardian website so it will have an educated readership who expect to understand hashtags and the references to Netflix.
Level 1 1–3	**Students will:** • **paraphrase or describe content of texts** • **misunderstand text or context.**	Text A is from a website so it contains hyperlinks and is written formally.

AO4: Explore connections across texts, informed by linguistic concepts and methods.		
Level marks	At this level	Indicative content
Level 5 13–15	**Students will:** • **evaluate the importance/significance/effect of connections found across texts.**	Both Texts A and B poke fun at the words and phrases they discuss. They both, however, do this for different reasons and with different effects. While Text A uses a degree of humour to highlight what is ultimately a serious point about what she sees as an unnecessary divide between neologisms coined to refer to male and female traits and the sexist undertones this process suggests are 'feminism's fault, naturally'. The start of Text B implies a degree of light-hearted derision for the rules which are being implemented around language in schools by using the somewhat archaic word 'admonished' in relation to five-year-old children and by pointing out that it is the volunteer girls who will 'police sexist attitudes' - a task which seems a little too much for the aforementioned five-year-olds. These contrasting uses of humour both serve to underpin the attitudes the texts take to their topics. Text B's choice of the word 'squad' evokes both military organisation, which seems disproportionate to the task, and the 'squads of girls' that seem to link to Text A's discussion of neologisms in whose meanings the 'subtlety has been lost'.
Level 4 10–12	**Students will:** • **explore connections between texts by linking language and context.**	Both Texts A and B use the examples of language they are discussing to demonstrate their views on the topic of language and gender. Text A maintains a lighthearted tone through the use of faintly absurd sounding portmanteau words, whereas Text B presents a more cynical view of the suggested necessity for language change it is reporting on. These representations are broadly in line with the publications for which they are writing in terms of political leanings and worldview.
Level 3 7–9	**Students will:** • **make connections across texts by identifying similar or different uses of language/content/ context.**	Both texts provide a range of examples of the lexis that they are discussing in terms of language and gender. In Text A there is a range of new blend words, which mostly sound a bit odd: 'guyliner', 'feminazi' and which are not often used in conversation, whereas in Text B there are only a few phrases referred to: 'man up', 'don't be a girl', which most people would already be familiar with and may have heard being used in everyday life.
Level 2 4–6	**Students will:** • **make connections at a literal level.**	Both texts give examples of the words and phrases that they are discussing, such as 'girlboss' and 'man up'.
Level 1 1–3	**Students will:** • **discuss relevant aspects of texts without making connections explicitly.**	Text A uses examples of the words it is discussing such as 'manspreading' and 'girlboss'. Text B talks about the phrases that schools are trying to stop from being used.

4.	Write a feature article about gendered language in which you assess the ideas presented in Text A and Text B and argue your own views. [30 marks]
	This question is marked out of 20 for AO2 and out of 10 for AO5. Both AOs should be consistently addressed throughout your answer so there will be overlap between them.
	Use these grids to focus on your level for each skill.

AO2: Demonstrate critical understanding of concepts and issues relevant to language use.	
Level marks	**At this level**
Level 5 17–20	Students will: • demonstrate a synthesised, conceptualised and individual overview of issues • evaluate and challenge views, approaches and interpretations of linguistic issues.
Level 4 13–16	Students will: • identify and comment on different views, approaches and interpretations of linguistic issues.
Level 3 9–12	Students will: • show detailed knowledge of linguistic ideas, concepts and research.
Level 2 5–8	Students will: • show familiarity with linguistic ideas, concepts and research.
Level 1 1–4	Students will: • discuss issues anecdotally without specialist linguistic knowledge.

AO5: Demonstrate expertise and creativity in the use of English to communicate in different ways.	
Level marks	At this level
Level 5 9–10	Students will: • use form creatively and innovatively • use register creatively for context • write accurately.
Level 4 7–8	Students will: • use form convincingly • show close attention to register, effective for context • show strong control of accuracy.
Level 3 5–6	Students will: • use form competently • use and sustain register, effective for context • show firm control of accuracy.
Level 2 3–4	Students will: • use form appropriately • use appropriate language for context • make occasional errors.
Level 1 1–2	Students will: • use form limited to simple elements • shape language broadly for context • make intrusive errors.

There are many possible responses to this question. Here is an example part of a possible answer:

It seems as though you can't get away from the topic of gender at the moment doesn't it? The pervasive trope, which keeps cropping up in everything from politics to sport, from newspapers to Facebook feeds, has become the subject du jour for any right-on, liberal campaigner to get behind and vent their snowflakey spleen. With the phrase 'man up' being banned on school playgrounds and any internet debate reducing itself to nothing more than frantically typed virtue signalling and who can 'check their privilege' first, hasn't it all gone too far? Well, frankly, no. No it hasn't. Anyone who uses the argument that we have currently got our second woman PM is wilfully ignoring the fact that we've never had a single female Chancellor of the Exchequer. For every 'SheEO' of a top company, there are thousands of women who are underpaid and undervalued in essential roles, and for every man who understands that there's nothing wrong with doing things 'like a girl', there are millions of others ready to tell him to 'man up'. Babies are socialised into their expected gender roles from the moment they are born (or even before – hello gender reveal parties!) and the language that surrounds this is an absolutely fundamental part of how society does this. However you feel about the Sapir-Whorf hypothesis, there is a grain of truth in the idea that the language we use and the language used about us frames the way in which we view the world. When Spender coined the term 'man made language' she certainly didn't see the opposite of 'man' as 'girl'; the fact that half the population are habitually referred to as children only serves to reinforce the idea that female is less than male. This idea is borne out by the condescending tone taken by Helena Horton in her article on governmental attempts to outlaw sexist language in schools. I will confess to having been baffled from the outset of her article, which appears to imply that schools working to prevent the kind of subtle (and not so subtle) gender stereotyping which leads to so few young women choosing to study STEM subjects is somehow making an undesirable fuss about nothing.

This partial response has strengths and weaknesses. It uses the source articles to support the points it makes and shows a strong command of written English with a sense of creativity. A full response at this level would suggest a Level 4 mark.

AO2: This is a partial answer that begins to draw links to linguistic theories such as the Sapir-Whorf hypothesis. A more developed answer would build on these and challenge different perspectives in the field of language and gender research. The response makes references to the ideas raised in the two source articles from Question 3 and begins to challenge some of the arguments presented.

AO5: This response shows a creative command of written English and strikes an appropriate tone for the required feature article style. There is a clear sense of an authorial viewpoint being set up and the political references are used judiciously to establish the writer as knowledgeable on the subject at hand.

Practice Exam 2

English Language

Paper 1: Language, the Individual and Society

Section A: Textual Variations and Representations

1.	Analyse how **Text A** uses language to create meanings and representations. **[25 marks]**
	This question is marked out of 10 for AO1 and out of 15 for AO3. Both AOs should be consistently addressed throughout your answer so there will be overlap between them.
	Use these grids to focus on your level for each skill.

AO1: Apply appropriate methods of language analysis, using associated terminology and coherent written expression.

Level marks	At this level	Indicative content
Level 5 9–10	Students will: • **apply linguistic methods and terminology, identifying patterns and complexities** • **apply different levels of language analysis in an integrated way, recognising how they are connected** • **apply levels of language analysis with rare errors** • **guide the reader.**	The frequent use of formal, high register lexis such as 'homage', 'myriad' and references to Xenophon indicate that the audience for this article is expected to be well educated and engaged with the topic in question. There is a pattern throughout the article of contrasting the 'constitutional royalty' who bore witness to the event with the 'TV royalty' who provided the entertainment, which forms part of a running theme about the 'unusual combination' of events. The discourse is rather detached, creating a generally formal reporting tone through always remaining in the active voice. This sense of detachment is occasionally allowed to slip when making reference to the Queen having worn ear plugs at a previous 'pop concert' – a piece of information that alters the tone of the discourse and encourages the reader to view the proceedings positively by creating a gently humorous, anecdotal rapport.
Level 4 7–8	Students will: • **apply linguistic methods and terminology with precision and detail** • **apply two or more levels of language analysis** • **apply levels of language analysis with occasional errors** • **develop a line of argument.**	The lexical choices that the writer employs throughout this article are frequently intended to highlight the 'unusual combination' of entertainments and events that took place. While the general tone of the article is detached and formal, the writer uses anecdotes such as the Queen's use of 'ear plugs' at a previous concert to suggest that the event was a positively received one. Lexis of a very formal register such as 'homage' and 'sated' is used by the author to reflect the tone of the event and the closing quote from Prince Charles, quoting Xenophon, reinforces this.
Level 3 5–6	Students will: • **apply linguistic methods and terminology consistently and appropriately** • **label features that have value for the task** • **label features with more accuracy than inaccuracy** • **communicate with clear topics and paragraphs.**	Horses are used and referenced throughout Text A. it is clear that this is because the Queen has a 'love of horses' and the writer has chosen to weave this into the text at levels from lexis to discourse. There are alliterative horse references: 'equine extravaganza', classical horse quotes: 'Xenophon's observation that "a horse is a thing of beauty"' and references to how certain guests fitted into the horsey line-up: 'president of the British Horse Society'. All of this goes together to create a semantic field of horses and equestrian references.

Level 2 3–4	Students will: • **use linguistic methods and terminology inconsistently and sometimes without value for the task** • **generalise about language use with limited/unclear evidence** • **label features with more inaccuracy than accuracy** • **express ideas with organisation emerging.**	The text uses the semantic field of horses and ponies: 'love of horses', 'horse-drawn Scottish state carriage'. This shows that the event was heavily focussed on horses and ponies and that this was because the Queen likes them so much. Horses are mentioned in almost every paragraph, creating a strongly horse-themed text.
Level 1 1–2	Students will: • **quote or identify features of language without linguistic description** • **present material with limited organisation.**	Text A uses lots of words and phrases about horses and ponies to show that there were lots of them there and that the Queen likes horses. This is repeated throughout the text to emphasise how important horses were at the celebrations.

AO3: Analyse and evaluate how contextual factors and language features are associated with the construction of meaning.		
Level marks	At this level	Indicative content
Level 5 13–15	Students will: • evaluate use of language and representations according to context • explore analysis within wider social and cultural contexts.	Text A uses a combination of alliteration, gentle humour and equine references to convey the appropriate level of formality and respect in its reporting of the Queen's 90th birthday celebrations. The use of humour is carried out with a very light touch as it would be inappropriate for a broadsheet publication to poke fun at the monarch and could be considered disrespectful which, in the context of reporting on her birthday celebrations, would be considered inappropriate by most of the readership of the article. The tone of respectful distance and some degree of reverence has been firmly established before the writer adds that 'There was no visible evidence of the Queen wearing ear plugs' and drawing attention to the fact that she apparently had done at a previous pop concert. This small inclusion of humour, which could be seen as being at the Queen's expense, suggests an attempt to lighten the tone of the article.
Level 4 10–12	Students will: • analyse how language choices create meanings and representations • analyse how aspects of context work together to affect language use.	By taking a fairly informal tone to report on a very formal event involving hundreds of horses and thousands of people, the author for Text A has created a sense that while the Queen is to be respected, she is not above reproach; the author therefore uses gentle humour, saying that 'There was no visible evidence of the Queen wearing ear plugs' as she watched the pop concert that was being put on in her honour. This suggests that the Queen might not have enjoyed the music and that she has previously been seen wearing ear plugs at similar events – an action that does not reflect well on the performers and could make the Queen look somewhat rude. Text A therefore represents the events as worthy of note but still 'human' amid all of the pageantry.
Level 3 7–9	Students will: • interpret significance of specific choices of language according to context • link specific language choices with an aspect of context.	Text A is written in order to inform and entertain the reader. It uses a mixture of language techniques such as alliteration and humour in order to describe the events at the Queen's 90th birthday celebrations. The use of alliteration is appropriate for the context as it adds to the description of the scene and the use of humour shows that the newspaper website it is published on wants to keep the tone of the reporting light and fairly informal.
Level 2 4–6	Students will: • identify distinctive features of language and significant aspects of context.	Text A uses some alliteration to introduce the description of what happened at the Queen's 90th birthday party: 'equine enthusiast', 'paraded and pranced'. It also gives a list of who came to the celebrations and of the entertainment that was put on. The text was published on a newspaper website, so the readers will have clicked on it and chosen to read it.
Level 1 1–3	Students will: • paraphrase or describe content of texts • misunderstand text or context.	Text A uses different techniques to get the reader's attention and to tell them about what happened at the Queen's 90th birthday party. It was written in a newspaper, so it will be a reliable source of information and it includes who went and what they did there: 'Helen Mirren' and 'a re-enactment of the Queen's life'.

2.	Analyse how **Text B** uses language to create meanings and representations.	**[25 marks]**

This question is marked out of 10 for AO1 and out of 15 for AO3. Both AOs should be consistently addressed throughout your answer so there will be overlap between them.

Use these grids to focus on your level for each skill.

AO1: Apply appropriate methods of language analysis, using associated terminology and coherent written expression.

Level marks	At this level	Indicative content
Level 5 9–10	**Students will:** • **apply linguistic methods and terminology, identifying patterns and complexities** • **apply different levels of language analysis in an integrated way, recognising how they are connected** • **apply levels of language analysis with rare errors** • **guide the reader.**	The main part of Text B only consists of three sentences. Two of these contain a far higher number of clauses and subordinate clauses than we would expect of a modern text. The second sentence, however, is comparatively short; this suggests that the use of a variety of sentence structures was part of the usual discourse for a descriptive text of this type at the time. The sentences deal with different individual issues and seem to be long and multi-claused because this adds to the descriptive element, creating a sense of immersion in the scene for the reader. The grammatical form of Text B demonstrates how the construction of meaning has changed over the course of the last 400 years.
Level 4 7–8	**Students will:** • **apply linguistic methods and terminology with precision and detail** • **apply two or more levels of language analysis** • **apply levels of language analysis with occasional errors** • **develop a line of argument.**	Text B's grammar shows the difference between the sentence construction standards of 1613 and those of today. The final sentence on the page contains multiple subordinate clauses and often uses commas to demarcate these: 'at the further end whereof, upon the Queenes approch, a Cynick appeared'. These sentence constructions may appear excessive to the modern eye but form a fundamental part of the descriptive style that the writer is using to create a narrative discourse.
Level 3 5–6	**Students will:** • **apply linguistic methods and terminology consistently and appropriately** • **label features that have value for the task** • **label features with more accuracy than inaccuracy** • **communicate with clear topics and paragraphs.**	The grammar of Text B shows that sentence construction in 1613 followed different standards to the ones we use 400 years later. The final sentence is the longest, with semicolons and colons being used to add on further clauses and keep the description of the grounds and the 'Cynick' entertainer going.
Level 2 3–4	**Students will:** • **use linguistic methods and terminology inconsistently and sometimes without value for the task** • **generalise about language use with limited/unclear evidence** • **label features with more inaccuracy than accuracy** • **express ideas with organisation emerging.**	Text B uses long grammatical constructions to add a lot of detail to the descriptions it gives the reader. The sentences are long and complex and use a large number of clauses.
Level 1 1–2	**Students will:** • **quote or identify features of language without linguistic description** • **present material with limited organisation.**	Text B uses a lot of very long sentences to build up a description of the house and the 'Cynick' who jumps out of the trees at the end.

AO3: Analyse and evaluate how contextual factors and language features are associated with the construction of meaning.		
Level marks	At this level	Indicative content
Level 5 13–15	Students will: • evaluate use of language and representations according to context • explore analysis within wider social and cultural contexts.	Text B relies heavily on adjectives and descriptive noun phrases to craft a mental image for the reader of the house, the entertainer and their surroundings 'mounted on the hill-side of a Parke, within view of Redding'. This is because the author cannot rely on a printed image to set the scene, so he must do so himself. The cultural context of the nobility in 1613 also means that Lord Knowles will be keen to describe, and boast a little about, the setting of his house when the Queen paid a visit. It seems therefore unexpected to read about the 'Cynick' who begins the entertainment upon Queen Anne's arrival as he is described as having 'his nakednesse [...] artificially shadowed with leaves'. This seems at odds with the formal tone and description set out at the start of the text and may have been crafted to excite the reader.
Level 4 10–12	Students will: • analyse how language choices create meanings and representations • analyse how aspects of context work together to affect language use.	In 1613 printing was still an expensive process, so the use of images was rare. This meant that writers had to be especially descriptive as they could not rely on illustrations to set the scene for them. This is why Text B relies so heavily on a description of the house 'fairely built of bricke', its surroundings 'within view of Redding' and the 'Cynick' who appears at the end of the passage wearing 'a false haire, blacke and disordered, stucke carelessely with flowers.' These descriptive passages and adjectives create a representation of the scene in which the entertainments for Queen Anne take place.
Level 3 7–9	Students will: • interpret significance of specific choices of language according to context • link specific language choices with an aspect of context.	The fact that printing limitations mean Text B does not contain any images means that the writer must make up for this by including detailed descriptions of the surroundings, people and events. This means that there are numerous examples of adjectives and noun phrases being used to build a descriptive piece: 'he wore a false haire, blacke and disordered, stucke carelessely with flowers'.
Level 2 4–6	Students will: • identify distinctive features of language and significant aspects of context.	Text B does not contain any pictures and therefore the writer relies on written description of events and surroundings to paint a picture for his readers. He describes the house as 'fairely built of bricke' and the man at the end as 'drest in a skin-coate' to help the reader understand what was happening.
Level 1 1–3	Students will: • paraphrase or describe content of texts • misunderstand text or context.	Text B uses lots of description to show the reader what the house looked like and how the 'Cynick' who jumps out of a tree to start the entertainment looks and what his costume is like.

3.	Explore the similarities and differences in the ways **Text A** and **Text B** use language.	**[20 marks]**
	This question is marked out of 20 for AO4.	

AO4: Explore connections across texts, informed by linguistic concepts and methods.

Level marks	At this level	Indicative content
Level 5 17–20	**Students will:** • **evaluate the importance/significance/effect of connections found across texts.**	The two texts employ markedly different levels of formality when describing the respective Queens and the surroundings and events to which they are referring. Text A creates a humorous tone 'no visible evidence of […] ear plugs' while remaining generally respectful. Text B, in contrast, uses only the most respectful and formal forms of reference to 'our most gracious Queen: Queene Anne'. This contrast demonstrates the different levels of esteem in which the royal family was held in the two time periods. When Text B was written in 1613 the role of the royal family was to rule and be in control of the country, whereas today the role is ceremonial. The modes of these two texts also have a significant effect on the ways in which language is used in them. While Text A will have appeared in the print version of the newspaper, it is also available online and because the Guardian is free to access, its readership is large and reaches a broad base. Text B, meanwhile, published only 150 years after Caxton brought the printing press to England, would have had a far narrower original readership – not least because so many fewer people could read to this level or had the resources to access such a publication. Despite this 400-year gap between their publication, Texts A and B demonstrate that the topic of royal events has always been newsworthy in the UK.
Level 4 13–16	**Students will:** • **explore connections between texts by linking language and context.**	Text A uses descriptive features to describe the celebrations put on for Queen Elizabeth's 90th birthday, using alliterative phrases such as 'equine extravaganza' and 'paraded and pranced' – this gives a sense of the pageantry of the occasion, which is mixed with some gentle humour about any 'sign of ear plugs' when the Queen watched a pop concert. This is in some contrast to the author of Text B, which treats Queen Anne's visit and the entertainment laid on as an opportunity to boast about how grand his home is and what it looks like, perhaps because the likely reader would be of a lower social standing and could be expected to be impressed by the description as – unlike the events of Text A that were 'televised live on ITV', the reader of Text B can only rely on a mental picture of the surroundings being created for them. This difference in the contexts in which the texts were published means that the writers' lexical choices are markedly different; in order to set the scene for the reader, Text B describes the house in detail as 'fairly built of bricke' and being 'mounted on the hill-side of a Parke', noun phrases that are rendered potentially unnecessary by the wider media coverage of the event Text A describes, leaving it to concentrate its lexical flourishes on describing the atmosphere at the 'equine extravaganza'.

Level 3 9–12	Students will: • make connections across texts by identifying similar or different uses of language/content/ context.	Text B demonstrates a good deal of respect for Queen Anne and gives a detailed description of the house where she is staying while the entertainments take place as part of her journey to 'Bathe' through 'Redding', using descriptive lexis such as 'mounted on the hill-side of a Parke' to demonstrate how grand the house is. The writer of Text A clearly has a reasonable degree of respect for the Queen but does not give such vivid descriptions of the setting when explaining how the celebrations took place, simply stating that they were at 'Windsor Castle'.
Level 2 5–8	Students will: • make connections at a literal level.	Both texts are about entertainment and celebrations that have been arranged in honour of the Queen at the time. In Text A the Queen's birthday celebrations are related in some detail with a list of who was there and what events were put on, while in Text B the full page only gets to the point where the Queen is arriving.
Level 1 1–4	Students will: • discuss relevant aspects of texts without making connections explicitly.	Text A is about the Queen's birthday celebrations and what happened, who was there and what they did. Text B is about Queen Anne visiting a Lord on her way through Reading to Bath.

Section B: Child Language Development

4.	'The use of questions has a significant impact on a child's acquisition of language.' Referring to Data Set 1 in detail, and to relevant ideas from language study, evaluate this view of children's language development. **[30 marks]** **This question is marked out of 15 for AO1 and out of 15 for AO2. Both AOs should be consistently addressed throughout your answer so there will be overlap between them.** **Use these grids to focus on your level for each skill.**

AO1: Apply appropriate methods of language analysis, using associated terminology and coherent written expression.

Level marks	At this level	Indicative content
Level 5 13–15	Students will: • **apply linguistic methods and terminology, identifying patterns and complexities** • **apply different levels of language analysis in an integrated way, recognising how they are connected** • **apply levels of language analysis with rare errors** • **guide the reader.**	In Data Set 1 Lucy's mother uses a number of different questions to prompt a dialogue with Lucy. She uses a mixture of open questions: 'What are you doing Lucy?' and closed questions: 'Are you turning it?' to elicit responses from her daughter. It would be reasonable to expect, in line with Bruner's ideas about open questions in Child Directed Speech (CDS) leading naturally to more developed answers with closed questions having the opposite effect for children past the two-word stage, that Lucy would give longer, more developed answers to her mother's open questions and shorter, one-word answers to the closed ones. This, however, does not seem always to be the case. In response to the open question 'What are you doing Lucy?', she gives a detailed answer: 'I want to go in the car', but the next open question she is asked: 'What are you going to do?' is met with the reply 'um', which suggests that Lucy does not have a ready response to her mother's attempt at conversation.
Level 4 10–12	Students will: • **apply linguistic methods and terminology with precision and detail** • **apply two or more levels of language analysis** • **apply levels of language analysis with occasional errors** • **develop a line of argument.**	Lucy and her mother demonstrate some elements of what Bruner expected from Child Directed Speech. When her mother asks a closed question Lucy always gives a short answer, however, when she asks an open question Lucy is sometimes able to give a longer response. At the age of two-and-a-half Lucy is at a crucial point in developing her responses and progressing through the telegraphic to the post-telegraphic stage. The use of questions seems to be supporting Lucy in this development.
Level 3 7–9	Students will: • **apply linguistic methods and terminology consistently and appropriately** • **label features that have value for the task** • **label features with more accuracy than inaccuracy** • **communicate with clear topics and paragraphs.**	The use of different types of question has an effect on the response a child can be expected to give. In Data Set 1 Lucy is asked a mixture of open and closed questions by her mother. Lucy mostly responds to open questions with more developed answers, but this is not always the case: 'M: What are you going to do? L: Um'. Bruner's theory of Child Directed Speech places a significant importance on the use of questions to encourage turn taking and develop a child's longer utterances.
Level 2 4–6	Students will: • **use linguistic methods and terminology inconsistently and sometimes without value for the task** • **generalise about language use with limited/unclear evidence** • **label features with more inaccuracy than accuracy** • **express ideas with organisation emerging.**	Lucy's mother uses open and closed questions at different points in Data Set 1. These different types of questions receive different types of answers from Lucy because she gives longer answers to the open questions and shorter answers to the closed ones.
Level 1 1–3	Students will: • **quote or identify features of language without linguistic description** • **present material with limited organisation.**	Lucy responds to her mother's questions with a range of answers. Some answers are shorter than others in response to the different questions her mother asks.

AO2: Demonstrate critical understanding of concepts and issues relevant to language use.		
Level marks	At this level	Indicative content
Level 5 13–15	Students will: • **demonstrate a synthesised, conceptualised and individual overview of issues** • **evaluate and challenge views, approaches and interpretations of linguistic issues.**	Through the question and answer structure, Lucy's mother provides a number of small clarifications and corrections of Lucy's developing speech patterns. For example, she repeats back certain words in which Lucy's pronunciation is non-standard and provides the accepted Standard English pronunciation: when Lucy says /tan/ her mother includes the word /kan/ in her response and when Lucy says /sjaɪjd/ her mother pronounces /slaɪjd/, with its challenging consonant cluster, as part of her next utterance. This is a less obvious use of the question and answer structure that would feed neatly into parts of both Skinner's behaviourist explanation of language acquisition and Chomsky's nativist approach as Lucy is having the 'truth' of her utterance recognised while the non-standard elements are being corrected and remodelled back to her. The fact that both of these theories can be supported in different ways here suggests that whilst both Skinner and Chomsky had valid ideas about some elements of child language acquisition, neither theory goes all the way to explaining the process.
Level 4 10–12	Students will: • **identify and comment on different views, approaches and interpretations of linguistic issues.**	Lucy shows an example of assimilation in her pronunciation, with the pronunciation of the consonant cluster at the beginning of 'slide' being changed to /sj/ to mirror the later /j/ sound in the word and minimise the difficult consonant cluster sound. This shows that Lucy is developing her phonological awareness and finding different strategies to help when she is faced with a challenging pronunciation.
Level 3 7–9	Students will: • **show detailed knowledge of linguistic ideas, concepts and research.**	Lucy finds some consonant sounds difficult to pronounce so she swaps them for different ones such as the /j/ sound being used in place of the /l/ sound. This is a common phenomenon, especially with consonant clusters, with the second sound being altered in order for the child to say it more easily.
Level 2 4–6	Students will: • **show familiarity with linguistic ideas, concepts and research.**	Lucy's phonological development is in progress and she drops some more difficult sounds and uses ones that are easier to pronounce instead. For instance, she says /sjaɪd/ instead of /slaɪd/.
Level 1 1–3	Students will: • **discuss issues anecdotally without specialist linguistic knowledge.**	Lucy is developing her language and mispronounces some of her words. This is because they are difficult to say, such as 'slide' and 'lift'.

5.	'Children's creative writing is more detailed than factual writing.'
	Referring to Data Set 2 and Data Set 3 in detail, and to relevant ideas from language study, evaluate this view of children's language development. **[30 marks]**
	This question is marked out of 15 for AO1 and out of 15 for AO2. Both AOs should be consistently addressed throughout your answer so there will be overlap between them.
	Use these grids to focus on your level for each skill.

AO1: Apply appropriate methods of language analysis, using associated terminology and coherent written expression.

Level marks	At this level	Indicative content
Level 5 13–15	Students will: • **apply linguistic methods and terminology, identifying patterns and complexities** • **apply different levels of language analysis in an integrated way, recognising how they are connected** • **apply levels of language analysis with rare errors** • **guide the reader.**	Minnie uses appropriate features of both writing types to convey her ideas. While her age and some accuracy features of her writing put her firmly in the preparatory stage of Kroll's written development stages, there are some features of Minnie's writing and her ability to differentiate between text types which suggest that she is in the consolidation stage already as she is able to link ideas and join clauses using conjunctions. Minnie broadly writes in a way that mimics speech patterns but her ability to switch between factual and fiction styles is clear in the constructions and levels of detail she employs.
Level 4 10–12	Students will: • **apply linguistic methods and terminology with precision and detail** • **apply two or more levels of language analysis** • **apply levels of language analysis with occasional errors** • **develop a line of argument.**	The level of detail present in Data Set 3 in comparison to Data Set 2 demonstrates that Minnie writes longer, more detailed pieces when she is writing creatively. She is clearly approaching the consolidation stage of writing as identified by Kroll and can differentiate between the requirements of fact and fiction texts. Data Set 3 shows that Minnie understands that fiction texts introduce characters: 'a girl and a boy' and use adjectives to describe the events that take place: 'amazing'. In contrast to this, Minnie is able to craft an appropriate factual text, using a list to state the different clubs she attends.
Level 3 7–9	Students will: • **apply linguistic methods and terminology consistently and appropriately** • **label features that have value for the task** • **label features with more accuracy than inaccuracy** • **communicate with clear topics and paragraphs.**	In Data Set 2 and Data Set 3 Minnie is writing for different purposes and fulfilling different functions as identified by Halliday. The texts were written within a few weeks of one another so it is unlikely that she has made major learning leaps in between them. This suggests that Minnie is able to choose how she crafts her language for different types of text.
Level 2 4–6	Students will: • **use linguistic methods and terminology inconsistently and sometimes without value for the task** • **generalise about language use with limited/unclear evidence** • **label features with more inaccuracy than accuracy** • **express ideas with organisation emerging.**	Minnie uses language differently to write her ideas down when she is writing a story and when she is writing an account of her hobbies. She uses longer, more detailed sentences and adds information to her characters to show what is happening in the story. In Data Set 2 she writes a list of the clubs she attends. This shows that she is writing for different purposes.
Level 1 1–3	Students will: • **quote or identify features of language without linguistic description** • **present material with limited organisation.**	Minnie writes differently when she is writing a factual text about the clubs she goes to. When she writes creatively she uses more words to show what is happening.

AO2: Demonstrate critical understanding of concepts and issues relevant to language use.		
Level marks	At this level	Indicative content
Level 5 13–15	Students will: • demonstrate a synthesised, conceptualised and individual overview of issues • evaluate and challenge views, approaches and interpretations of linguistic issues.	Minnie alters her sentence structures in order to provide longer, more detailed sentences when she is constructing a creative piece of narrative. She also uses the classic 'Once upon a time' opening, which she will be familiar with from traditional fairy tales. I would argue that Data Set 2, while shorter and simpler in its structure, is an equally appropriate example of its text type to Data Set 3 as it shows the use of a centralised, capitalised heading and contains a list of the 'clobs' that she attends. Minnie also makes use of logical phoneme–grapheme links to support her developing grasp of orthography.
Level 4 10–12	Students will: • identify and comment on different views, approaches and interpretations of linguistic issues.	Grammatically, Minnie uses capital letters with accuracy at the start of sentences in both texts. Interestingly, she capitalised the first letter of 'Isaac' but not 'poppy'. This could be due to being more familiar seeing the first name written down, or because she is familiar with producing a capital 'I' when the word stands alone. Minnie structures the discourse of Data Set 3 to show that she is writing a story by using the traditional opening 'Once upon a time'; this suggests that she is aware of the structures used to construct narratives.
Level 3 7–9	Students will: • show detailed knowledge of linguistic ideas, concepts and research.	Minnie uses full stops with consistent accuracy. She presents both lists and sentences with multiple clauses in Data Sets 2 and 3 but she is still developing her understanding of commas and their uses. In Data Set 2 there is a mark attached to the word 'recorder' that may have been intended as a comma and would be correctly placed but this is unclear. Minnie will have been attending school for at least a year now and so will have had formal instruction in some aspects of punctuation.
Level 2 4–6	Students will: • show familiarity with linguistic ideas, concepts and research.	Minnie is developing her written accuracy in terms of spelling, punctuation and grammar. She is able to use full stops correctly and does so at the ends of sentences in both texts.
Level 1 1–3	Students will: • discuss issues anecdotally without specialist linguistic knowledge.	Minnie's written accuracy is developing. She uses a high number of correct standard formations in her writing.

Practice Exam 2

English Language

Paper 2: Language, Diversity and Change

Section A: Diversity and Change

1.	Evaluate the idea that social groups use language in order to exclude others.
	This question is marked out of 10 for AO1 and out of 20 for AO2. Both AOs should be consistently addressed throughout your answer so there will be overlap between them.
	Use these grids to focus on your level for each skill. [30 marks]

AO1: Apply appropriate methods of language analysis, using associated terminology and coherent written expression.

Level marks	At this level
Level 5 9–10	Students will: • apply linguistic methods and terminology, identifying patterns and complexities • apply different levels of language analysis in an integrated way, recognising how they are connected • apply levels of language analysis with rare errors • guide the reader.
Level 4 7–8	Students will: • apply linguistic methods and terminology with precision and detail • apply two or more levels of language analysis • apply levels of language analysis with occasional errors • develop a line of argument.
Level 3 5–6	Students will: • apply linguistic methods and terminology consistently and appropriately • label features that have value for the task • label features with more accuracy than inaccuracy • communicate with clear topics and paragraphs.
Level 2 3–4	Students will: • use linguistic methods and terminology inconsistently and sometimes without value for the task • generalise about language use with limited/unclear evidence • label features with more inaccuracy than accuracy • express ideas with organisation emerging.
Level 1 1–2	Students will: • quote or identify features of language without linguistic description • present material with limited organisation.

AO2: Demonstrate critical understanding of concepts and issues relevant to language use.	
Level marks	At this level
Level 5 17–20	Students will: • demonstrate a synthesised, conceptualised and individual overview of issues • evaluate and challenge views, approaches and interpretations of linguistic issues.
Level 4 13–16	Students will: • identify and comment on different views, approaches and interpretations of linguistic issues.
Level 3 9–12	Students will: • show detailed knowledge of linguistic ideas, concepts and research.
Level 2 5–8	Students will: • show familiarity with linguistic ideas, concepts and research.
Level 1 1–4	Students will: • discuss issues anecdotally without specialist linguistic knowledge.

There are many possible responses to this question. Here is an example part of a possible answer:

R B LePage said that we speak the language of the social group with which we wish to be identified. If we accept this as true then it stands to reason that by using the same language features as a method of inclusion for group members, those who use different language features would be identified as being outside the group. Shared speech patterns and lexis can put people at ease. Milroy's Belfast study shows that being considered part of a group is crucial in terms of people altering their language use in front of strangers. Labov's study in Martha's Vineyard shows that using language to signal belonging is a powerful social tool, with a younger generation pointedly using the local dialect and accent features to mark themselves out from those who were new to the area.

This opening paragraph makes a strong case for the writer's understanding of language research and how different studies can be linked together to form a bigger picture of a language trend. This response, developed in full, could reach a high Level 4.

AO1: A clear line of argument is established, and different language levels are noted as being crucial for identifying the patterns that will support a rounded response to the question. This could be strengthened by a close analysis of the different language levels that are at play when language is used as a social tool to include or exclude.

AO2: This introduction makes a very clear overview of a number of language studies and their relevance to the question. The reference to the Martha's Vineyard study provides a clear link to the concept of language signalling group membership and a purposeful use of it to exclude and so makes a judicious choice for analysis. This could be strengthened by drawing in studies that the writer could challenge and potentially argue against.

2.	Evaluate the idea that prescriptive attitudes are detrimental to language development. [30 marks]
	This question is marked out of 10 for AO1 and out of 20 for AO2. Both AOs should be consistently addressed throughout your answer so there will be overlap between them.
	Use these grids to focus on your level for each skill.

AO1: Apply appropriate methods of language analysis, using associated terminology and coherent written expression.

Level marks	At this level
Level 5 **9–10**	**Students will:** • **apply linguistic methods and terminology, identifying patterns and complexities** • **apply different levels of language analysis in an integrated way, recognising how they are connected** • **apply levels of language analysis with rare errors** • **guide the reader.**
Level 4 **7–8**	**Students will:** • **apply linguistic methods and terminology with precision and detail** • **apply two or more levels of language analysis** • **apply levels of language analysis with occasional errors** • **develop a line of argument.**
Level 3 **5–6**	**Students will:** • **apply linguistic methods and terminology consistently and appropriately** • **label features that have value for the task** • **label features with more accuracy than inaccuracy** • **communicate with clear topics and paragraphs.**
Level 2 **3–4**	**Students will:** • **use linguistic methods and terminology inconsistently and sometimes without value for the task** • **generalise about language use with limited/unclear evidence** • **label features with more inaccuracy than accuracy** • **express ideas with organisation emerging.**
Level 1 **1–2**	**Students will:** • **quote or identify features of language without linguistic description** • **present material with limited organisation.**

AO2: Demonstrate critical understanding of concepts and issues relevant to language use.	
Level marks	At this level
Level 5 17–20	Students will: • demonstrate a synthesised, conceptualised and individual overview of issues • evaluate and challenge views, approaches and interpretations of linguistic issues.
Level 4 13–16	Students will: • identify and comment on different views, approaches and interpretations of linguistic issues.
Level 3 9–12	Students will: • show detailed knowledge of linguistic ideas, concepts and research.
Level 2 5–8	Students will: • show familiarity with linguistic ideas, concepts and research.
Level 1 1–4	Students will: • discuss issues anecdotally without specialist linguistic knowledge.

There are many possible responses to this question. Here is an example part of a possible answer:

There are many parts of life, corners of the internet and indeed newspaper letters pages which demonstrate that prescriptive attitudes towards language use are as prevalent as ever. Many linguists would, however, argue that while it is important to have an accepted standard for a language in terms of ease of communication, there is little value or realistic hope of achieving a fully prescribed standard usage for a living language. Perhaps the most shining example of resistance to language change and a prescriptive attitude is the Académie française, whose main purpose is to preserve the French language, and which has a reputation for rejecting neologisms – particularly borrowed words. David Crystal would disagree with this approach: in his words, 'All languages change. They have to.'

This opening paragraph is rather casual in tone, but it makes relevant, supported references to a number of different language concepts and issues. If this line of discussion in relation to the question were developed into a full response with reference to the notes below it could reach a low Level 4.

AO1: The final line of this paragraph sets out a line of argument that can be developed through the full response. There is clear and accurate use of linguistic terminology that directly links to the question. This could be substantially improved by making specific reference to key constituents of language and how prescriptive attitudes may be brought to bear on them.

AO2: This response shows a clear understanding that vastly different opinions exist on the topic of language change but makes a clear argument that the more prescriptive attitudes are held by those who are not linguistic researchers by contrasting 'corners of the internet' with references to David Crystal. There is plenty of potential here for a robust discussion of the topic.

Section B: Language Discourses

3.	Analyse how language is used in Text A and Text B to present ideas about how young people use language. In your answer you should:
	• examine and similarities and differences you find between the texts
	• explore how effectively the texts present their views. **[40 marks]**
	This question is marked out of 10 for AO1, out of 15 for AO3 and out of 15 for AO4. All AOs should be consistently addressed throughout your answer so there will be overlap between them.
	Use these grids to focus on your level for each skill:

AO1: Apply appropriate methods of language analysis, using associated terminology and coherent written expression.

Level marks	At this level	Indicative content
Level 5 9–10	**Students will:** • **apply linguistic methods and terminology, identifying patterns and complexities** • **apply different levels of language analysis in an integrated way, recognising how they are connected** • **apply levels of language analysis with rare errors** • **guide the reader.**	Isabelle Kerr distances herself from belonging to her own demographic by emphasising her ignorance of the 'appalling' neologisms that they are introducing into the English language. Despite going to great pains to establish this distance between her and the 'young generation' she consistently includes herself later in the article by consistently using the inclusive pronouns 'we', 'us' and 'our'. This shows that she is not rejecting her membership of the group but seeking to place herself both within it and above it through use of complex vocabulary such as 'promulgate', a term that would be in the expected vocabulary for the typically well-educated Telegraph reader.
Level 4 7–8	**Students will:** • **apply linguistic methods and terminology with precision and detail** • **apply two or more levels of language analysis** • **apply levels of language analysis with occasional errors** • **develop a line of argument.**	Isabelle Kerr uses a range of grammatical structures and discourse features to distance herself from the 'pitiful emblems of the current young generation's contribution to language'. After having seriously insulted the young generation, she uses short sentences to establish distance between herself and them when she admits they are 'My generation. I am 20.' and goes on to avoid membership of this linguistic group by stating that she 'actually had to Google' the word 'twerk' to find out what it meant.
Level 3 5–6	**Students will:** • **apply linguistic methods and terminology consistently and appropriately** • **label features that have value for the task** • **label features with more accuracy than inaccuracy** • **communicate with clear topics and paragraphs.**	The writer of Text B uses an element of humour in her discourse as she uses several examples of the type of language she says she dislikes in her opening sentence such as 'srsly', 'unlike' and 'vom'. This shows that she is taking a relatively informal approach to the topic and suggests that she does not take it too seriously.
Level 2 3–4	**Students will:** • **use linguistic methods and terminology inconsistently and sometimes without value for the task** • **generalise about language use with limited/unclear evidence** • **label features with more inaccuracy than accuracy** • **express ideas with organisation emerging.**	The writer of Text B uses some lexis and some grammar in her article. She writes about how bad the types of words that young people use are. She particularly hates words like 'twerk' and 'selfie'.
Level 1 1–2	**Students will:** • **quote or identify features of language without linguistic description** • **present material with limited organisation.**	The writer of Text B shows how she feels about how young people use language by using negative words to describe it, such as 'pitiful'.

AO3: Analyse and evaluate how contextual factors and language features are associated with the construction of meaning.		
Level marks	At this level	Indicative content
Level 5 13–15	**Students will:** • **evaluate use of language and representations according to context** • **explore analysis within wider social and cultural contexts.**	Schopen constructs an article that uses just as much overstatement in her takedown of youth vocabulary as she claims the young people in question are doing themselves in their 'having overblown emotional responses to commonplace events'. The Guardian online has a wide, educated, typically liberal readership and is not behind a paywall. In the heading, subheading and final line of her article, Schopen uses some of the phrases she claims to so detest: 'I can't even', 'can you not', indicating a sense of irony that would be appropriate and likely well received by her readers. This creates an informal tone, which indicates that her primary purpose is to entertain. She separates herself completely from 'the kids' who habitually use these language forms, yet confesses to 'allow[ing] [herself] an ironic "lolz" occasionally'. This blurs Schopen's stated age divide in the language use but suggests that older age groups use the neologisms in a different way to 'the kids'.
Level 4 10–12	**Students will:** • **analyse how language choices create meanings and representations** • **analyse how aspects of context work together to affect language use.**	The writer of Text A presents herself as a professional writer who dislikes the proliferation of new terms that young people have brought into the English language. Schopen is writing for the Guardian online, which has a wide and generally educated readership. Schopen uses very clear, forceful language to express her dislike of terms such as 'bae' and 'can you not', saying that she hates 'to see language butchered like this' and that it is 'to [her] horror' that she found out bae had been added to the OED. This creates a comedic effect that makes her point clear but does not take itself too seriously.
Level 3 7–9	**Students will:** • **interpret significance of specific choices of language according to context** • **link specific language choices with an aspect of context.**	The writer of Text A is presenting her point of view on new words and phrases used by young people. She clearly feels that language is 'evolving in the wrong direction', by which she means it is getting worse. She uses an informal tone and gives examples of the types of words and phrases that she disagrees with, such as 'bae', 'I can't even' and 'all the feels'. She is writing for an online newspaper in the context of an opinion article that has a title that may be clicked on by the same young people who use the language she dislikes.
Level 2 4–6	**Students will:** • **identify distinctive features of language and significant aspects of context.**	Text A is written by someone who is older than the people she is talking about, so she doesn't use the same language as them and doesn't understand it.
Level 1 1–3	**Students will:** • **paraphrase or describe content of texts** • **misunderstand text or context.**	Text A is about how the author does not like the types of language that young people use.

AO4: Explore connections across texts, informed by linguistic concepts and methods.		
Level marks	At this level	Indicative content
Level 5 13–15	**Students will:** • **evaluate the importance/significance/effect of connections found across texts.**	Despite sharing a disdain for words such as 'bae' and 'selfie', the authors of these two articles approach the problem in different manners. Text A's author Fay Schopen uses hyperbole to distance herself from the language of an age group younger than she is (despite confessing to allowing herself 'an ironic "lolz"') whereas Isabelle Kerr takes an apologetic tone that blames her own generation while trying to absolve herself of responsibility by making the strength of her dislike known.
Level 4 10–12	**Students will:** • **explore connections between texts by linking language and context.**	The two texts are united by their authors' distaste for neologisms such as 'bae' and 'twerk', which have been brought to prominence by young people. They are, however, approaching the topic from different perspectives, as Schopen is older than the age group that uses the words she so hates, while Kerr is aged 20 and therefore takes an apologetic tone as she sees her generation as being the cause of the problem.
Level 3 7–9	**Students will:** • **make connections across texts by identifying similar or different uses of language/content/context.**	Both texts are written to be viewed online and therefore will have self-selecting audiences who have chosen to read them due to an interest in the topic. Both authors use their articles to explain how much they dislike new words that are being introduced into the language by young people. They use expressions of 'horror' to show how 'pitiful' they believe the neologisms to be.
Level 2 4–6	**Students will:** • **make connections at a literal level.**	Both the authors of Text A and Text B share a dislike of new words that have recently entered the English language due to being used by young people. They say that they are 'loathsome' and 'appalling'.
Level 1 1–3	**Students will:** • **discuss relevant aspects of texts without making connections explicitly.**	Text A shows that the author does not like the language used by young people. The writer of Text B is a 20-year-old who does not think that the new words being added to the dictionary are reflecting well on the young people who use them.

4.	Write an opinion article about young people's language use in which you assess the ideas presented in Text A and Text B and argue your own views. **[30 marks]**
	This question is marked out of 20 for AO2 and out of 10 for AO5. Both AOs should be consistently addressed throughout your answer so there will be overlap between them.
	Use these grids to focus on your level for each skill:

AO2: Demonstrate critical understanding of concepts and issues relevant to language use.

Level marks	At this level
Level 5 17–20	Students will: • **demonstrate a synthesised, conceptualised and individual overview of issues** • **evaluate and challenge views, approaches and interpretations of linguistic issues.**
Level 4 13–16	Students will: • **identify and comment on different views, approaches and interpretations of linguistic issues.**
Level 3 9–12	Students will: • **show detailed knowledge of linguistic ideas, concepts and research.**
Level 2 5–8	Students will: • **show familiarity with linguistic ideas, concepts and research.**
Level 1 1–4	Students will: • **discuss issues anecdotally without specialist linguistic knowledge.**

AO5: Demonstrate expertise and creativity in the use of English to communicate in different ways.	
Level marks	**At this level**
Level 5 9–10	Students will: • use form creatively and innovatively • use register creatively for context • write accurately.
Level 4 7–8	Students will: • use form convincingly • show close attention to register, effective for context • show strong control of accuracy.
Level 3 5–6	Students will: • use form competently • use and sustain register, effective for context • show firm control of accuracy.
Level 2 3–4	Students will: • use form appropriately • use appropriate language for context • make occasional errors.
Level 1 1–2	Students will: • use form limited to simple elements • shape language broadly for context • make intrusive errors.

There are many possible responses to this question. Here is an example part of a possible answer:

Is there a problem with the type of language young people use? For some, yes, for others (most notably the young people who use the language themselves) no, of course not. For every generation there is something they are blamed for as change takes place – votes for women, rock 'n' roll music, mini-skirts, text speak – all drew outrage from older generations when they first appeared on the scene, and this generation's sticking point seems to be the vocabulary they use. Words such as 'bae', 'twerk' and 'lolz' are habitually ridiculed for reasons that many judgmental commentators struggle to put their finger on; is it because they are focussed on appearance and social media interactions, because they overuse hyperbole, or simply because they are new? In my opinion, there is a hefty dollop of prescriptivism and no small amount of ageism in the mix here, for every generation has introduced new words to the language. Outside the fields of science and technology, young people are the biggest linguistic innovators we have and while not every neologism will stand the test of time, in fifty years this will be the language of the elderly, having 'all the feels' about pictures of their grandchildren. As David Crystal says, 'every part of language changes' and there will always be those who look to avoid this, but try as they may they 'won't stop the change taking place'.

This opening paragraph of a response clearly addresses the question and shows that the writer had a strong command of written English. A continued response at this standard would find a Level 4 mark.

AO1: There is clear reference to different opinions on the use of language by young people and this is supported by reference to Crystal's writings on the subject of language change. Both of the source articles from question 3 are referenced in passing. This could be improved by a developed analysis of the language levels on which the changes young people make are operating.

AO2: This piece shows a creative, accurate use of the English language, with appropriate register and vocabulary selection for the task set.